Parenting

A Practical Manual in Anticipatory Guidance

by

Shu Shum, M.D., M.B.A., F.A.A.P.

D1279750

Parenting
A Practical Manual in Anticipatory Guidance

Copyright © 2005

Amarillo Pediatric Associates, Inc.
(806) 358-8526

DISCLAIMER

The information contained in this publication is intended to supplement the knowledge of health care professionals. This information is advisory only and is not intended to replace sound clinical judgment or individualized patient care. The author disclaims all warranties, whether expressed or implied, including any warranty as to the quality, accuracy, safety, or suitability of this information for any particular purpose.

ISBN 0-9729583-4-7
Library of Congress Control Number: 2005921053

Cover design by Joyce Moore
Chinese title calligraphy by Nien-Chu Shen

It is important for you to ask your pediatrician or physician about his or her philosophy concerning the care of your children.

Contents

About Myself...7
About This Book 8
Acknowledgments...9

PART I

My Philosophy of the Practice of Pediatrics 13

PART II

Your Pregnancy 19
Your Newborn...27
Feeding Your Newborn...43

PART III

The Two-Week-Old 59
The Two-Month-Old..67
The Four-Month-Old...75
The Six-Month-Old..83
The Nine-Month-Old...91
The One-Year-Old 99
The Fifteen-Month-Old 107
The Eighteen-Month-Old 115
The Two-Year-Old 123
The Preschooler: The Three- to Five-Year-Old.......................................133
The Six- to Nine-Year-Old 147
The Early Adolescent Years 155
The Mid-Adolescent Years 171
The Late Adolescent Years...185

PART IV

Anticipatory Guidance 197

Parenting Skills 211

PART V

Emergencies 223

Sick Visits... 225

Office Waiting Time.. 229

Recommended Immunization Schedule... 230

Footnotes on Immunization Schedule 232

Catch-up Immunization Schedule.. 234

Growth Chart-Birth to 36 Months-Length & Weight - Boys.................. 236

Growth Chart-Birth to 36 Months-Length & Weight - Girls 237

Growth Chart-Birth to 36 Months-Head Circumference-Boys.............. 238

Growth Chart-Birth to 36 Months-Head Circumference-Girls 239

Growth Chart-2 to 20 Years-Stature & Weight for Age-Boys 240

Growth Chart-2 to 20 Years-Stature & Weight for Age-Girls............. 241

Growth Chart-2 to 20 Years-Body Mass Index-Boys............................ 242

Growth Chart-2 to 20 Years-Body Mass Index-Girls 243

Growth Chart-2 to 20 Years-Weight for Stature-Boys 244

Growth Chart-2 to 20 Years-Weight for Stature-Girls.......................... 245

PART VI

Suggested Reading 249

About Myself

I graduated from the University of Hong Kong, Faculty of Medicine, in 1971 and began my residency in pediatrics at Queen Mary Hospital, the teaching hospital of the University of Hong Kong. I immigrated to the United States in 1973 and trained in pediatrics at Tulane University in New Orleans, where I served as a resident in pediatrics for two years. I left Tulane in 1976 upon the completion of my residency.

During a fellowship program at the Developmental Pharmacology Branch of the National Institute of Child Health and Human Development at the National Institutes of Health in Bethesda, Maryland, I researched the effects of drugs on the fetus and explored the mechanisms of toxicity of different drugs and chemicals in experimental models.

After completing my fellowship, I moved to Aberdeen, Washington, and set up my pediatric practice. I practiced there for three years. In 1980, I joined the staff of the Texas Tech University Health Sciences Center in Amarillo, Texas, as an Assistant Professor in Pediatrics and Assistant Professor in Pharmacology and Therapeutics. I held this position until I decided to set up my private practice of pediatrics in Amarillo, Texas.

I was certified by the American Board of Pediatrics in 1978 and the American Board of Medical Toxicology in 1980. I was elected to be a Fellow of the American Academy of Pediatrics, a Member of the American Academy of Clinical Toxicology in 1981, and a Fellow of the American College of Medical Toxicology in 1996.

About This Book

For the past twenty years as a primary care pediatrician, I have learned from my patients and their families. I wish to write about my experiences and my interaction with them to inform future pediatricians that primary care pediatrics is a very rewarding specialty, not necessarily financially, but emotionally and spiritually. The smiles of an infant, the greeting of a toddler at the local mall, and the hugs of a teenager all provide immeasurable joy. As you watch human beings grow and mature into successful, righteous persons in society, the immense satisfaction that one feels is beyond whatever possible financial gain may be found in other medical specialties.

Expecting parents can use this book to guide them through the task of parenthood. It will give them a fair idea of what to expect at each stage of development so they can be informed and prepared for their youngster when they reach that particular stage of formation. This book will provide parents guidance and information, just like a manual that they may have gotten when they acquired any new item in their everyday life.

Growth is a continual process that we all learn from. It is our experience that guides us through the hard times and allows us to enjoy the good times. I hope this book will serve its function and is worth the effort of going through page by page. One may need to re-read it a few times to master the skills and information one needs in this changing society. However, the basic principles of loving, caring, nurturing, providing, guiding, and forming a youngster will not change. Your concern and your efforts will be rewarded handsomely as you watch your youngster mature into a pillar in our society, a person that you can be proud of in the years to come. Good luck!

In order to avoid cumbersome gender reference to the youngster, the pronoun "he" will be used, until the later chapters when specific gender is being discussed.

Acknowledgments

I dedicate this book to my family. I learned a lot from my children, Elaine, Lucy, and John. They were my unknowing experimental subjects. I tested my theories on them and watched their response, taking notes on what worked and what failed. I appreciate my wife Serey's support throughout all these years of experimentation. I am sure there were moments of doubt and uncertainty as she watched our children grow. It is through their support, encouragement, and stimulation that I have had the chance to complete this book. I dedicate it to my parents who demonstrated and taught me parenting and the caring, nurturing nature of my profession. I dedicate it to the fond memory of my grandmother. She taught me to be a sensitive person, to look out for other people's needs, and to never forget about giving. Lastly, I dedicate this to all my patients and their families who taught me the vast majority of the information that I write about in this book.

I also wish to thank all my teachers, mentors in the different facets of pediatrics, particularly Professor Elaine Fields, Professor G.M. Kneebone, Dr. Wei-Ying Lui, Dr. Alice Chau, Dr. Anita Li, Dr. K.Y. Wong, Dr. K.H. Wei, Dr. David Su and the staff of The University of Hong Kong, Faculty of Medicine, Department of Pediatrics; Dr. Harry C. Shirkey, Dr. Norman Woody, Dr. Hannah Woody, Dr. William Waring and the staff of Tulane University, Department of Pediatrics; Dr. Daniel Nebert of the Developmental Pharmacology Branch of National Child Health and Human Development, National Institutes of Health, and Dr. William O. Robertson of the University of Washington. To them, I owe much for their teaching and modeling as teachers and mentors, influencing the formation of my thinking and conception of pediatrics and child rearing.

I hope this book serves its purpose.

part

My Philosophy of the Practice of Pediatrics

The field of pediatrics involves the care of a developing, dependent individual, nurturing that individual to maturity. It is total advocacy of this individual that makes pediatrics exciting. If the health care professionals in the field of pediatrics, together with the parents and other caretakers of the youngsters, do their jobs appropriately, we will have a much more harmonious society. All the pain and suffering that we encounter in our lifetime can be minimized if we plan ahead to avoid undesirable outcomes. After all, the goal of parenting is to nurture an individual to be a happy, healthy, well adjusted, and successful person in society.

Pediatrics is not just caring for sick children; it has a much broader scope. The practice of pediatrics (from ancient Greek, pedo meaning child and iatrikos meaning physician) is quite different from orthopedics (ortho meaning right or straight and pedo meaning child, also from ancient Greek). Pediatrics is total advocacy for the youngster, instead of the mere practice of healing the sick or righting the wrong.

I believe that God creates all human life. Conception begins life. The mother's womb nurtures the fetus for nine months. Through the birth process, the child comes into the world as a member of the family and society. It is this fruit of matrimony that we are called to nurture and to guide for years to come.

Before a couple decides to have children, they should examine the vocation of parenthood. Parenthood is a vocation -- a long-term commitment to the love and caring of the child, his nurturing and guidance to independent, successful adulthood. It calls for a sacrifice of personal freedom, financial security, and conveniences for the parents. Yet, a child is a gift from God. Children will provide heavenly joy for their parents. The laughter, the tears, the fun, and the joy are all part of the continuous process of growing up. This is the ultimate fruit of matrimony and the fulfillment of God's command to inhabit the Earth. It is desirable that both parents sit down and examine every point of parenthood in detail to ensure that every child is a wanted child - well cared for, well loved, and deserving.

When a couple decides to have children, it is important for them to visit their future obstetrician and pediatrician before conception. You may outline your future plans to them, so that they may provide you their professional opinions on various aspects of pregnancy and child rearing. There are lists of precautions your doctor may provide for you. You may not know many of these facts that may adversely affect your future family. By the time you conceive your child, it may already be too late. This situation applies to genetic diseases that you may carry, drugs and chemicals that you may be taking, and physical agents like heat or radiation that may cause damage in early pregnancy. You should begin taking nutritional supplements, like minerals and vitamins, particularly folic acid, calcium, and iron.

It is interesting to note that an expecting young lady spends six to eight sessions in her prenatal birthing classes with her husband, anticipating and preparing for the labor process which normally lasts only ten to twelve hours. Yet, seldom do you hear about the same couple preparing for the caring and nurturing of their youngster for the next eighteen years! When attempts are made to start such a parenting class, one meets with resistance from all concerned because our society does not realize the importance of such preparation. Local hospitals, physician's offices, churches and other children's advocacy groups should organize these classes. With the involvement of professionals, such classes can be successful in focusing on the importance of this preparation for parenthood so that children grow up with the desired expectation of success in society.

If you have any family history of inherited diseases, please let your pediatrician know so you can find out the risk factors and make an informed decision. Drugs, chemicals, irradiation, and infections may affect the unborn child. If you are currently on a drug, exposed to a chemical, or suffering from an infection, please let your doctor know so he or she can provide the facts for you, particularly before you decide to have children. However, many facts may not be known to the medical profession. Each pregnancy can serve as an opportunity to explore the unknowns if you wish. Keep a good diary, record your observations - what you are being exposed to and what you may be consuming. This record may yield important information when it is analyzed in the future.

Prepare your home environment. Pesticides, herbicides, household chemicals, and fire retardants may all affect your unborn child. Pets may also carry occult infections that may adversely influence your pregnancy. Fish, birds, cats, and many other household pets may be hosts to parasites and/or fungal, bacterial, or viral infections that may harm your unborn child.

Once you desire to have children, you should start to take the necessary steps to ensure a positive outcome of your decision. You can start to prepare physically, emotionally, and financially for your children. You will need to have a broad scheme instead of focusing on the minor details of starting a family. You can seek input from your family, friends, ministers, and other persons whose opinions you value in forming such a plan. You will also need to make some personal adjustments in your routines and your habits to accommodate the coming of your children.

It is wise to start making a plan for your family. Family planning is a necessary step for all of us. One can start with what you and your spouse both desire. How many children? How far apart? How to make the living quarters suitable for the family? Obviously, you do not need to have everything you want before you start a family, yet it is advisable to go through the exercise and be prepared. At times, blessings come by the basketful; you may have twins or triplets. You just have to prepare for any circumstance that may happen and still accept it with grace. Accept help if you need to. It is not a sin to ask for help if you are in a position that is out of your control. Planning is human; fulfilling the plan is the will of God.

For each child, parents are encouraged to create a master profile for that child. In addition to properly nurturing and guiding your youngster, you need to prepare for the interaction of your child with you, your family, and your neighborhood. Write down specific goals and achievements that you desire. Record the superfluous traits you may want to avoid. This serves as a "blue print" when you try to guide and form your youngster. Sure enough, your youngster will interact with you, the parents! He may manipulate his mother to fight with his father; he may want to manipulate his father or mother to fight with his teachers in school. He may fight with his siblings to get his parents' attention. With a "blue print" in your hands, you can avoid some arguments with your spouse, since this "blue print" is crafted by both of you conscientiously. You may also solicit input from grandparents, friends and ministers who may have significant influence on your child's well being when you are building the idea of a "blue print." These subcontractors will be excited to implement your "blue print" if they have input into the plan.

Please do not focus on material goods for your family. One can be reassured that you cannot buy all the necessary things ahead of time. One does not need to be rich to be a parent. Instead, children need love, caring, nurturing, and, most importantly, time, guidance, and patience. Make your schedule suit your children. After all, you, the parents, are the ones who want them. The children are there for both of you.

PART

II

Your Pregnancy

When a couple decides to have children, the lady should start to take vitamin supplements, particularly folic acid. When you notice the first missing period, you may be in early pregnancy. It may already be too late for folic acid to prevent neuro-tube defects in your fetus. You may want to visit your dentist prior to your pregnancy . Let him know that you are planning to get pregnant. Tooth decay and gum disease may cause problems for you and your baby during your pregnancy. Your dentist will provide dental prophylaxis for you and guide you throughout your pregnancy. Try to quit smoking and avoid passive smoking. Cigarette smoke contains chemicals that may harm you and your unborn child. Your fetus may not get the appropriate amount of oxygen and nutrients from you when you are smoking, particularly during the first weeks of your pregnancy. Cigarette smoking may cause you to have a miscarriage or your unborn child may not develop normally. Cigarette smoking by the mother or exposure to passive cigarette smoke are known risks for the development of sudden infant death syndrome. It is never too late to quit smoking!

Pregnancy is divided artificially into three stages - the three trimesters of pregnancy. During the first trimester, you may have an uneasy feeling, particularly in the morning, with nausea and vomiting. Morning sickness is normal for early pregnancy. Try to eat small, frequent meals of healthy food. Trust your obstetrician or your family doctor. He or she will guide you through this, with or without the use of drugs. Start prenatal care as soon as you know you are pregnant. You may choose your obstetrician or family practice physician. If you choose an obstetrician, you will also need to choose a pediatrician for your baby. You should start your prenatal vitamins and your calcium supplement.

Communicate freely with your doctor on how you feel so he or she can help you effectively. You may feel the tightening of your breasts, pain when going to the bathroom to urinate, or you may have to void more frequently. These may just be symptoms of pregnancy. Do not assume that you have a urinary tract infection and start taking medicine. Check with your obstetrician or family doctor so they can culture the urine, do a pregnancy test, and make sure everything is all right.

About 10-15% of all pregnancies end up in spontaneous abortion. This may be a natural process or a pathological process that warrants further investigation. Let your obstetrician or family doctor know so he or she can form a professional opinion for you. Again, drugs, chemicals, heat, irradiation, and infections may affect the unborn fetus adversely in the first trimester. Your doctor may be able to determine any underlying conditions that may have caused the miscarriage. Some of these conditions are curable. A thorough gynecological examination at this point may identify any pathological conditions and may be able to prevent subsequent heartbreak and future miscarriages.

Please keep an accurate, detailed journal daily, particularly during early pregnancy. Record how you feel that day; what drugs you may be taking, your diet, and your body temperature. You should keep a diary or notebook during your whole pregnancy recording how you feel that day; what drugs you may be taking, your diet, and your body temperature. Your doctor will greatly appreciate this. Good food, fresh air, sunshine, appropriate exercise, and adequate rest are all important as soon as you find out that you are pregnant. Drink lots of water, milk, and fruit juices. Avoid excessive doses of caffeine in coffee, tea, and sodas. Maintain a balanced diet with appropriate grains and cereals, fruits, and vegetables. You need proteins and fatty acids, but try to limit fatty foods and sweets. You should avoid alcoholic beverages all together. Fetal Alcohol Syndrome is a preventable, pharmaco-genetic disease. If you develop a fever, record the temperature and let your obstetrician/family doctor know. This elevated temperature may signal an infection. However, not all elevated body temperature in a person signifies an infection. Strenuous exercise may elevate your body temperature! Try to avoid hot tubs, Jacuzzis, and saunas because even these artificial means of elevating your body temperature may affect your developing fetus adversely, with some long term, undesirable consequences.

During the second trimester of your pregnancy, you start to feel the baby move inside your womb. Your abdomen enlarges, particularly towards the end of your second trimester. You should wear loose, comfortable clothing that can be purchased in any maternity shop or department store. If you start to have spotting or other vaginal discharge, please let your obstetrician or family doctor know immediately so they can advise you appropriately. Organ formation is mostly completed; however, the fetus is still susceptible to infections and other damaging factors that may invade the intrauterine environment. It has been shown that during this stage of formation, a fetus may suffer a stroke as a result of maternal drug use. You should be careful about your own environment since passive smoking from your friends or relatives may adversely affect you and your fetus.

Starting late in the second trimester and at the beginning of the third trimester, you may feel periodic contractions of your uterus. These contractions are normal. However, your uterus may be very sensitive. To avoid premature labor, you should stop your activity when you have a contraction and rest for awhile. Normal contractions will stop spontaneously, and you can resume your activity. You should contact your obstetrician or family doctor immediately if the contractions continue, particularly if they are associated with vaginal discharge, amniotic fluid leakage, or bleeding. Do not wait until premature labor is fully established and beyond what modern obstetrics can offer.

Even if prematurity results, it is not your fault. Sometimes premature labor is simply unavoidable. However, with the advances in modern medicine, the care of a premature newborn is much improved. Neonatology is a special branch of pediatrics, specializing in caring for sick newborns. A neonatologist is a specialist in pediatrics who devotes all the working hours caring for sick newborns. Your physician may consider transferring your premature infant to the care of a neonatologist, if necessary. Your pediatrician will normally resume the primary care duties when the premature baby is discharged from the neonatal intensive care unit.

During the third trimester, you should try to exercise more and start your child birth classes. You may often feel tired, and your doctor's appointment may get be hectic. You will need a lot of rest. When you have free moments, start to prepare your nursery, gather your supplies, and make the final touches to welcome your newborn. If your maternity hospital offers parenting classes, this is a good time to attend these classes with your husband so that both of you will be on the same page with regards to your youngster. These classes may help you, your children, and your family for years to come.

A car seat is essential. Every car ride should be a safe ride, including the ride that brings your precious newborn home. The car seat should be properly installed. It should be certified by the Department of Transportation. It does not need to be costly. Some hospitals have programs that help you pay for the car seat if you cannot afford to buy one.

A crib should be prepared. The mattress should be firm and snugly fit the crib. Soft, natural fiber mattresses increase the risk of sudden infant death and should be avoided. If a bumper pad is to be used, it should also fit snugly into the crib so that the infant cannot be trapped between the bumper pad and the slats. The slats should be less than two and a quarter inches apart so that the infant's leg cannot slip through and get twisted. The slats should be painted with nontoxic paint free of any lead pigment since most older infants and toddlers chew on the slats.

You may want to consider an intercom to monitor your infant, particularly at night, when you want to listen to the noises or movements of your infant. A smoke detector installed inside the nursery is an essential investment. A carbon monoxide detector should also be installed in the living quarters. These items will alert the caring adult to rescue the infant in case of fire or carbon monoxide leakage.

You may be accustomed to the movements and kicks of your fetus by now, but if you notice a sudden change in these movements, please let your obstetrician/family doctor know. It may be normal, or it may signify a problem is developing inside your womb. Inform your doctor, let the doctor monitor your fetus.

If you find that the fetus is not moving at all, it is an obstetrical emergency. You should contact your doctor immediately. A proper physical examination needs to be done to evaluate the well-being of the fetus and determine whether there is any need for further intervention and management.

Towards the end of your pregnancy, you may find that your abdominal girth gradually drops. This is due to the engagement of the fetal head into your pelvis. You will find it easier to breath. Some fetuses may not engage until after the onset of labor. This is also normal.

Breastfeeding is the natural form of feeding an infant. You do not need to prepare your nipples as they are naturally prepared during pregnancy. Avoid excessive stimulation of your breast tissues, it may cause your uterus to contract or initiate an untimely labor process.

The third trimester is also a good time for the expecting couple to draw up a plan for their baby, the "blueprint" of nurturing and guiding the formation of this fruit of matrimony. You can discuss and write down your fantasies, your fears, your ideal human being, the good qualities from both sides of the families, the things you want to avoid, and the shortcomings you do not want to pass on to the next generation. You can invite the future grandparents, friends, ministers and relatives to participate in the planning sessions since they may have significant influence on the formation of this future personality. If they are a part of this "planning committee," it is more likely they will help you fulfill your dream than to say that it is "just your parent's crazy idea," and carry on a different agenda for your youngster in the future.

In the first place, as you can see, it is much easier to correctly form a person's mentality instead of reforming or rehabilitating a criminal. After all, no parent wants to have a criminal. You can use this "blueprint" to instruct any of your subcontractors- be they teachers, baby-sitters, friends or relatives who might influence the development of this future pillar of society. You can also wave this "blueprint" at your youngster later on, telling him that you will not let him manipulate you; that you have thought it through while he was still in-utero. This will avoid many unnecessary arguments between the parents when confronted by their children later on. The principles of loving, caring, nurturing, providing, and supporting the youngster will not change. You can always modify your "blueprint" during the formative years to fit your specific needs and concerns, remembering your goal as parents that you want your youngster to grow up happy, healthy, well-adjusted, self-confident, independent and successful in society.

This "blueprint" can be a very powerful tool in dealing with your children. It is not that the parents do not have good intent, but children manipulate their parents all the time so much so that parents can lose their prospective. No parent wants a son to sit behind bars in prison; no parent wants a daughter to be a prostitute; no parent wants to have violence in the neighborhood; no parent wants to have addicted sons or daughters; no parent wants to have seven trillion dollars of national debt; no parent wants criminals to be free and roaming. It is up to us, parents of our future generations, to correct the current mistakes in our country. No politicians or government can mandate the formation of our children.

With a "blueprint" in your hands, particularly after you have carefully crafted it, you can guide and nurture your youngsters with your conscience so that they become the leaders and masters of the future society. After all, this is what parents wish; they only need to develop ways to achieve it. Obviously, this "blueprint" is not cast in stone; you can modify it as it becomes necessary. After careful thought and deliberation, parents can modify their plans. This is much better than having no plan at all. Surely, this is the most important task for every expecting parent to complete because the well-being of the future society depends on these future leaders for years to come.

Your Newborn

Enjoy your newborn infant. Your newborn expects you to love, care for, cuddle, talk to, and play with them all the time. Newborn infants demand total care from feeding, bathing, and diaper changes to psychological care and attention to their feelings and needs. Learn to communicate with your newborn.

The newborn infant sees, hears, smells, and tastes. Your infant will let you know when he is hungry, upset, uncomfortable, happy or satisfied. The only communication skill a newborn has is crying and fussing. You will need to learn the meaning of his communication. Be observant. Try to find out what your newborn needs instead of plugging up a crying infant with a breast, bottle, pacifier, or simply ignoring him. Soon, you will learn to appreciate the different meanings of your youngster's cry and discontent. Crying is not harmful to your baby. Crying effectively expands the lungs and encourages their development. The lungs will continue to grow and develop until your youngster is seven years old! Find out why your infant cries. His cry carries a message. The message is important. Please do not just treat the symptom and ignore the message.

The newborn period is an excellent time for your infant to learn to tolerate his frustration. Tolerance of frustration is one of the most important tasks every person needs to master in life. A newborn cannot do any harm to anyone anywhere when he is frustrated. He will learn that being frustrated at certain times is a fact of life that he needs to master and tolerate. It is extremely important for parents to learn that providing opportunities for your infant to learn to tolerate their frustrating moments is as crucial as feeding and nurturing their infants. Tricks to soothe a frustrated infant when you cannot find a proper reason for his frustration exist. Talk to your baby; sing to him; read to him; and spend time cuddling and holding him. You may want to visit with your doctor to find out some of these tricks and, at the same time, ensure that your infant is not sick and you may not know it.

An infant sleeps most of the time during the day and is awake at night. This is actually an adaptive phenomenon. During the third trimester of your pregnancy as your uterus became bigger when your fetus grew, the uterine wall hugged the fetus. When you stood up and walked around, your uterus entered a semi-contraction tone. Your fetus felt the tightness, and this caused him to relax and fall asleep. At night when you were lying down, your uterus relaxed because the pull of gravity on your uterus and its contents was being supported. The relaxed uterus provided more room for your fetus to stretch. If you were awake, you would feel that your fetus kicked and moved more during the nighttime than during the day. So, in-utero, the fetus slept during the day and was awake at night. This carries forward into the early postnatal period. Gradually, the baby will adopt a more traditional sleeping pattern (normally between two and three months of age, and sometimes as late as six months of age). You can facilitate this learning process. You need to teach your baby to sleep at night by keeping your baby awake during the daytime! Keeping your infant awake during the daytime is good for both you and your infant. You want to enjoy your infant during your waking hours. The infant needs to learn to stay alert during the day so that you can spend meaningful, quality nurturing time with him. Keeping your infant awake during the daytime is not being mean to the infant. You are teaching him that he needs to be alert to learn during the daytime and sleep at night.

You can facilitate a smooth transition to keeping the infant awake during the daytime simply by exercising your newborn, stretching him, and not letting him go to sleep much during the day. You can also breastfeed the baby as often as every 60 to 90 minutes from about six or seven o'clock in the morning to about ten or twelve o'clock at night. Your infant needs to be breastfed ten to twelve times per day during early infancy. This frequent feeding makes the transition from continuous feeding in-utero to three meals a day as an adult much easier. Infants do not eat three meals a day! You need to feed your newborn small, frequent meals.

Do not over-feed your infant. Obesity is an avoidable illness with all its complications and long term consequences. Infants come with a built-in sucking reflex. If you offer a bottle of formula to an infant, the infant will suck even if he is not hungry. The appropriate amount to feed a bottle-fed infant is two and a half ounces per pound of body weight per twenty four hours, dividing that amount by ten if you feed your infant ten times or by twelve if you feed your infant twelve times per day.

Breastfeeding will not over-feed your infant. You should nurse your infant ten to twelve times per day, keeping your infant awake most of the day. By simply emptying your breast frequently and drinking enough fluid, you will build up your breastmilk supply. Human infants have thrived on breastmilk alone for millions of years. You produce colostrum for the first two to three days after your delivery. It will take four to six weeks for your breastmilk to mature. The milk slowly transitions to mature milk. Be patient with yourself and your baby. You will have enough breastmilk for your baby. There are factors that may affect your breastmilk. If breastfeeding hurts or if you have sore nipples, contact your physician or lactation consultant. Breastfeeding should not hurt! Visit and discuss with your doctor any problems you are having to see if you can correct them before you conclude that you cannot nurse your infant.

Newborn infants enjoy rhythm because they have been listening to their mothers' heartbeat and placenta blood flow sounds for nine months. Music or rhythm will be soothing to a frustrated infant. They also enjoy rhythmic motions because they have been rocked for nine months by the pulsations of the mother's arteries in-utero. Smooth, rocking movements will calm frustrated, crying babies, provided their immediate needs are met (feeding, wet diaper, etc.). Musical rhythm may also help a developing brain. Classical music may even improve the mathematical skills of a youngster later on during the school years.

Skin Care

Babies do not require daily baths. In fact, frequent baths may result in dry, scaly skin. Your baby should be sponge bathed until the umbilical cord falls off and the stump heals. Use mild soap or simply use warm water to wash your baby. DO NOT use soaps with perfumes, deodorants, or antibacterial agents because they will sensitize or irritate your infant's skin. DO NOT use oils, creams, and lotions because they may plug the sweat glands. Most newborns have dry, scaly skin. This is because all fetuses are effectively soaked in a tub of warm water inside their mothers' wombs for nine months. Thus, the newborn skin looks like the skin of a "dish-pan" hand. Do not be afraid that there is something wrong. The smooth baby skin that you see in magazine advertisements will come in the next six to eight weeks. As mentioned before, oil and lotion are designed to keep moisture on the skin; however, during the first six to eight weeks, a baby's skin needs to adapt to postnatal life in a dry environment. Thus, oils and lotions are not necessary and may actually be harmful, delaying the natural process of adaptation. Besides, these chemicals can penetrate the skin at this age since the barrier function of the skin is not mature yet and may accumulate in the baby's body for a very long time.

When the umbilical cord has fallen off and the stump is dry and healed, you may immerse the baby in water for bathing. Use a sink or an infant bathtub, and use lukewarm water. ALWAYS CHECK THE WATER TEMPERATURE WITH YOUR HAND BEFORE PUTTING THE INFANT IN THE WATER. It is a good idea to turn your hot water heater to the low setting if your have not done so before your infant comes home. Do not shampoo your baby girls' hair in the bathtub because the soap bubbles or shampoo in the bathtub water may irritate the mucus membranes of her vagina, causing vaginitis or urinary tract infections. These same soap bubbles will burn and sting the conjunctival sacs of her eyes.

Use a soft washcloth to wash the baby and a soft towel for drying. Do not use cotton swabs to clean the ears. Wash the ears with a wash cloth. Ear wax (cerumen) is normal and protective. You can remove earwax if necessary.

There are commercially available wax-removal kits or ear drops to soften the wax and facilitate the drainage. You can use them once or twice a week depending on the amount of wax available.

You may treat mild diaper rash with ZINC OXIDE OINTMENT or CALAMINE LOTION which are inexpensive and easily purchased. Try to avoid baby powder. **The powder may get into the vaginal area of baby girls causing significant irritation. It may get into the urethral area of baby boys.**

Head

The shape of babies' heads vary with the type of delivery and the length of labor. The swollen areas that have been there since birth will eventually round out. The molding area of the scalp (caput succedaneum) may exaggerate the presenting part of a vertex delivery. This is normal. It requires no extra attention other than keeping the area clean. Some babies develop cephalhematomas following hard labor processes. It is not necessary to do anything about them. It is actually harmful to massage or puncture them. They will eventually resolve and be incorporated into the shape of the skull. At times, when you pass your hand over the cephalhematoma, you may feel a cracking sensation underneath the scalp. You do not need to be frightened for you are not cracking the baby's skull. These are small, complex organic-calcium crystals that are dropping in the cephalhematoma. In most cases, the cephalhematoma will be resolved by two to three months of age, incorporating into the rest of the skull bones.

Many babies develop scaly, waxy crusts over their scalp. This is called "cradle cap" or "seborrhea." Washing with a soft brush such as a soft toothbrush, hairbrush, comb, or washcloth, will usually loosen the scales and remove them. Special cleansers may be recommended for you to use by your doctor.

Eyes

The baby's eyelids may at first be puffy. There may be a yellowish discharge. This discharge is usually due to an eye ointment routinely put in the baby's eyes at birth. There may be other causes as well so ask your doctor if you notice any eye discharge. Newborns frequently do not focus their eyes well and their eyes may even cross at times. Usually, this improves with age and is of little significance. If you notice such crossing and you are concerned, please let your physician know so that he/she may examine them to be certain it requires no treatment. You may also notice areas of blood stain in the "whites" of your baby's eyes. These areas are the result of broken blood vessels on the covering of the eyeball during the birth process. They will resolve in 3-4 weeks and will become yellow before disappearing completely. About one out of three infants may have a clogged tear duct at birth. You can help by massaging the tear duct area while you are feeding the baby. At times, there may be whitish or yellowish discharge coming out of the eyes; please let your doctor know so that appropriate steps can be taken to determine if the eye is infected or simply has a clogged tear duct.

Breasts

Many babies (male and female) have swelling in one or both of their breasts. Their breasts may have a milk-like secretion coming from them. These swellings are due to the mother's hormones while the baby was in her womb. Since the hormonal stimulation stopped at birth, the swellings will subside spontaneously requiring no therapy. Do not squeeze or massage the breasts. This may damage the tiny ducts inside the breasts or may introduce infection that can cause mastitis in the babies.

Vaginal Discharge

Most female newborn infants will have a creamy vaginal discharge. Some may have small amounts of bloody vaginal discharge during the first week of life. This bloody vaginal discharge is actually a mini-menstrual period resulting from the withdrawal of the maternal female hormones after the birth process. No treatment is necessary; simply keep the vaginal area clean with a wet wash-cloth. Most of the diaper wipes contain alcohol that may irritate or burn the vaginal area during this period. You may start using baby wipes once the vaginal discharge has subsided.

Umbilicus and Care of the Cord

The navel or umbilical cord is the stump left after cutting the long cord connecting the baby to the placenta in your womb. It will dry up, become hard, and fall off during the first three weeks of life. A few drops of blood should cause no alarm when the cord falls off. DO NOT let the cord get wet. Do not immerse the baby in water for a bath until the cord stump has fallen off and the umbilicus has healed. Do not clean with soap and water. You may clean the cord with rubbing alcohol. Notify your pediatrician if the cord stump area becomes gooey and/or foul smelling. Clean the cord stump with rubbing alcohol until it is fully healed. The cord area needs to be cleaned after every diaper change. You can use a cotton-ball soaked with rubbing alcohol. Squeeze the cotton ball over the cord so the alcohol soaks the base of the cord. The alcohol will not burn the cord since the umbilical cord itself does not contain any nerve fibers. However, if the alcohol starts to burn the infant umbilical area, it normally indicates that inflammation of the surrounding skin has already started. This needs to be distinguished from the coolness the infant may feel from the evaporation of the rubbing alcohol. If there is any redness or inflammation around the umbilical cord stump area, you need to inform your doctor. Your infant will need to be examined for the possibility of an umbilical cord infection.

If the area around the umbilical cord bulges when the baby cries, an umbilical hernia is present. Such hernias are common in African American infants. This type of umbilical hernia poses no danger to the child and, unless the hernia is very large, it will go away spontaneously in the first several years of life, requiring no therapy. Do not use an umbilical binder. Putting binders on the umbilicus when there is a hernia does not affect the hernia, but may result in skin rashes. As the infant's abdominal muscles develop, the tight, fibrous tissue between the muscles will seal off the umbilical hernia.

Legs

Most babies are bow-legged as a result of their position in the womb. Some babies' feet turn in while others turn out. Only rarely is therapy necessary. If you are concerned about your baby's feet, let your doctor know. You can help your infant by gently exercising his feet, stretching his knees, and flexing and abducting his hips. These exercises will strengthen your baby's legs.

Testes

Some male infants will not have their testicles in their scrotal sacs at birth. If such is the case with your baby, let your doctor know and he will examine your infant and discuss the finding with you. You may not feel the testicles within the sac. This is because some infants pull their testicles out of their scrotal sacs when touched around the groin area. The testes retract into the inguinal canal. This is normal.

Circumcision may be done in the newborn period. There are several different methods of circumcision. Some use a plastic bell. This tiny plastic device comes off by itself around the seventh day after the circumcision is done. Please do not push the plastic bell back towards the shaft of the penis as this may interfere with the circulation of the penile shaft and do harm to the tissue. There may be a piece of Vaseline gauze around the penile shaft if your doctor used another method to do the circumcision. That piece of Vaseline gauze may be taken off after a few hours. The wound area should be kept lubricated with lots of Vaseline or Neosporin ointment. This will prevent the wound from sticking to the diaper, irritating the wound during diaper changes. You may find a whitish or yellowish discharge on the glans of the penis. This is normal and is not pus. This does not indicate an infection. However, if you are concerned, please let your doctor know. Any wound can become infected. If you have doubts, please ask someone who may know. Do not wait until it is too late.

Circumcision is not a necessary operation. It is done as a custom rather than a medical necessity. There are advantages to being circumcised, yet there are complications as well. There are contraindications for circumcision. If your doctor advises you not to have a circumcision done on your infant, please accept that. Your doctor may have good reasons for that advice. After all, you can always have your son circumcised later.

Groin

Report any swellings above the groin area to your physician. Swollen glands cause most of these swellings, requiring no therapy. However, hernias requiring therapy may also occur in the groin area.

Sleep

Newborn babies sleep most of the time between feedings. It is not uncommon during the first few weeks of life for a newborn to sleep up to twenty hours a day. Mature newborns enjoy sleeping on their abdomen (prone) because this posture makes them feel as if they are embraced. It also decreases gastric emptying time. Even if they spit up, they will not choke on their vomitus. Recently, there have been reports of an association between prone sleeping and sudden infant death syndrome. Other factors that are associated with sudden infant death syndrome are: soft mattress or bedding material, swaddling the infant with blankets, a heated environment during cold winter days, and an upper respiratory infection. The prone posture may still be acceptable when the baby is awake; however, the American Academy of Pediatrics recommends the supine (sleeping on their back) position as the preferred sleeping position. The left lateral position (laying the babies on their left side) is an acceptable alternate position.

Often babies jerk or act startled during their sleep without any reason at all. Sometimes such activity occurs in response to loud noises. Such jerking or acting startled is normal.

Babies do not need to have a heavy blanket or tight clothing. During the day or at night, whatever clothing you feel comfortable in will be comfortable for your baby. Babies often kick off their covers. A warm sleeper or a sleeping bag type of blanket is appropriate during the cold, winter months.

Infants should not be put to sleep on water beds, sofas, soft mattresses, or other soft surfaces. This increases the risk of sudden infant death syndrome. Soft materials, like pillows, quilts, comforters, and stuffed toys should be kept out of an infant's sleeping environment.

As discussed before, newborn infants like to sleep during the day and stay awake at night. This is because during the late gestational period gravity pulls the uterus when the mother walks around. This increases the uterine tone, hugging the fetus tight, and prompting the fetus to go to sleep. However, at night when the mother is lying down, the uterine pull is supported and the uterus relaxes. The fetus is awakened because there is more room to move around. Most expectant women will tell you that they feel more fetal movements during the nighttime than during the day. It is important for you to keep your baby awake and up most of the day, particularly before the feeding time, so that your baby learns to sleep at night. This is not being mean to the baby. By keeping your baby awake during the daytime, your baby will learn to sleep through the night more quickly. This can be a big relief for everybody concerned in your household, particularly if you have older children that may need to go to school during the day.

While you are playing with your baby and when your baby is awake, a certain amount of tummy time is recommended for developmental reasons. A good exercise is to place your infant on an inflated beach ball, letting your infant move his arms and legs freely, rotating the infant from side to side. This activity is encouraged, especially prior to each feeding. Your infant may not like these exercises initially, but you will soon find that your infant learns to enjoy these movements as these movements enhance his development.

Regurgitation (Spitting up)

This is a normal phenomenon for newborns. Newborns spit up because the muscle between the esophagus and the stomach is not fully developed and the sphincteric function of that junction is incompetent at that age. They will spit up a little or have "wet burps" of undigested milk around their mouth or on the bed sheet. This is not due to a milk allergy. Burp your baby after each feeding. Sit him in an infant seat at a 45^0- 60^0 position for at least an hour before you lay him or her down to sleep in the crib.

Excessive spitting up is not normal, particularly if you notice there is a decrease in urination. You need to let your doctor know if you change less than six to eight wet diapers a day. Excessive regurgitation is also not normal when your infant is fussy after spitting up or when your infant fails to gain weight appropriately. Inform your doctor about your concerns. Let your doctor make the appropriate diagnosis and manage your infant.

Care of Diapers, Clothes, Bedding, Towels

You should wash your baby's clothing and bedding regularly. The choice of detergent is probably not important, but rinsing the clothes, bedding, and towels thoroughly after each washing is very important. Use bleaches and fabric softeners if desired, but again, thorough rinsing is essential. Try to double rinse all laundry. Please do not use sheet-type fabric softeners. They have strong irritants and are not suited for a newborn's skin. They may irritate the infant's delicate skin causing contact dermatitis.

Disposable diapers are perfectly acceptable. However, in hot summer weather, your doctor will advise frequent diaper changing because the plastic outer parts seal the diaper area resulting in sweating and rash formation. This also applies to the ultra-absorbent type of disposable diapers - you may not even be able to tell that the diaper is wet! Change these diapers often. The same recommendation applies when using cloth diapers with plastic pants for your small infant.

Room Temperature

The room temperature should be above 57° F in the winter months. This is an adequate temperature for a mature newborn. As for premature babies, the neonatologist normally will not release them from the newborn intensive care unit if they cannot keep their body temperature in a 57° F room. Some bluish discoloration of the hands and feet is normal. This does not mean that they need more clothes or need a hot water bottle which can be dangerous for a newborn. This is physiological. Acrocyanosis is common in newborn infants. This happens because of the vasomotor tone of the infant and the relative immaturity of the peripheral circulation in an infant. This also explains why the infant's hands and feet are cold most of the time. Bluish discoloration on the mucous membranes is discussed at length below under "cyanosis."

Please let your pediatrician know immediately if any of the following symptoms occur:

1) Jaundice- yellowish discoloration of the skin and eyes. Blood carries oxygen to the various tissues of the body. Specifically, the hemoglobin in the red blood cell carries the oxygen. Incidentally, "anemia" is the name of the condition that exists when there is too little hemoglobin in the blood cell. Babies are born with high hemoglobin levels and their hemoglobin levels drop immediately as they adjust to life outside their mothers' wombs. Destroyed red blood cells release their hemoglobin into the blood stream. The body acts on the free hemoglobin and breaks it down to bilirubin in the liver. The liver cells conjugate the bilirubin with another chemical. The "conjugated" bilirubin is soluble in water. The urine and stool eliminate this conjugated form of bilirubin from the body. This conjugation function of the newborn's liver is not fully mature at birth. Therefore, it is unable to handle the load of bilirubin presented to it. The bilirubin builds up in the blood stream and in the tissues of the body. As the level of bilirubin accumulates, the skin of the baby becomes yellow, stained by the buildup of bilirubin. This condition is call neonatal jaundice (jaundice means yellow). Sometimes breastmilk contains a chemical that inhibits the conjugation function of the

liver, thus breastfeeding the infant may increase the bilirubin level. This can also result in neonatal jaundice. Usually the jaundice from the simple, immature liver function peaks at about the fifth or sixth day of age and is not high enough to warrant any worry. Very high bilirubin levels can, however, result in permanent brain damage. Thus, if the bilirubin levels get too high, treatment is necessary. Usually, all that is necessary is to place the baby under indirect sunlight by the window or under a special fluorescent lamp to break apart the bilirubin into soluble fragments secreted in the bowel movements by the infant. If your baby's bilirubin level is abnormally high, your pediatrician will request that you sign a permission form for an exchange transfusion. In severe cases, an exchange transfusion, where fresh blood is "exchanged" for the baby's blood, may be necessary.

2) Cyanosis- a bluish discoloration of a baby's hands and feet when he is cold is normal in any newborn. However, a bluish discoloration of the lips and tongue of a newborn is not normal. Again, let your doctor know immediately if your baby's lips and tongue are blue. Your pediatrician will determine the cause and take appropriate measures to establish the correct diagnosis and determine the appropriate management. This is particularly true when cyanosis is accompanied by difficulty breathing or gasping for air. Some babies may be blue without having difficulty breathing. The bluish discoloration can be from a circulating pigment, methemoglobin. It is best to let your doctor examine your baby and determine the etiology of this situation.

3) BREATHING STOPS - THIS IS ALWAYS AN EMERGENCY! Call 911 for an ambulance IMMEDIATELY. While waiting for the ambulance, breathe for your baby by blowing air through his mouth and nose at the same time at the rate of approximately 40 breaths per minute. If you have an extra pair of hands, determine whether the baby has a heart beat. If there is no heartbeat or a palpable pulse, massage the baby's heart using your thumb and finger to squeeze his chest wall. When the ambulance arrives, please let the trained professionals help you. They have received specific training in resuscitation and you can trust them. They will let your physician know what has happened, and a doctor will meet you within minutes at the

hospital and determine how to further treat your baby. Time is important. Interruption of breathing for just a few minutes may harm your baby. Please do not waste time. Call 911 immediately for an ambulance. In this situation, every second counts.

4) Coughing - this is a rare symptom for a newborn and young infant. When it happens, it usually signifies a lung disease rather than a cold. Please inform your physician so that he or she can examine your baby and diagnose the cause of his cough. You can expect your physician to run tests or x-rays if he or she thinks it is necessary after examining your baby.

5) Temperature - a rise in body temperature in a newborn or young infant is definitely abnormal and demands immediate attention. Babies younger than eight to ten weeks have a lower ability to combat and localize an infection. If your baby has a temperature (a rectal temperature reading above 100.5° F), notify your pediatrician immediately. Please expect your doctor to examine your baby to determine the cause of the elevated body temperature. Again, your pediatrician may perform blood work, urine tests, x-rays of the chest, and/or a spinal tap to locate the infection and treat it properly. Expect your infant to be admitted to the hospital for observation and management for at least a few days, until all the culture results are available.

6) Vomiting - this is an abnormal symptom in the newborn. Should your baby vomit after feeding or without a feeding, inform your physician immediately. He or she will examine the baby to determine the cause of the vomiting. Over-feeding is a common reason for vomiting, particularly if you are bottle-feeding. Since babies are used to being fed continuously inside your womb, they may not stop eating even if they are full. The general rule is to feed your baby ten times a day, at an interval of 90-120 minutes during the daytime, from about six o'clock in the morning to about eleven o'clock in the evening. The volume of food in that twenty-four-hour period should be around two and a half ounces of formula per pound of the baby's body weight. This will provide enough nutrients and fluid for your infant. If you are breastfeeding, you will not over-feed your baby. If you have a strong let-

down reflex, your breastmilk may initially flow too quickly into your baby's throat and cause him to choke and vomit. If this situation occurs, break the suction by inserting one of your fingers in the grove between your breast and your baby's mouth. Let the milk flow into a cup or towel. Once the milk flow slows, reattach the baby. This way, the milk will flow more slowly into your baby's mouth and can be swallowed more evenly.

7) Diarrhea - after the meconium stools and the transitional stools, babies will have semi-liquid stools that are yellowish and curd- like in nature if they are breastfeeding. In the newborn period, they may stool after each feeding. This is normal and is termed gastrocolic reflux. However, if your baby's stool is watery or contains flecks of mucus, it is not normal and you should call your pediatrician immediately. Depending on the situation, your pediatrician may give you advice over the phone or may ask you to bring the baby in to be examined to determine the cause of the diarrhea. DO NOT GIVE KEOPECTATE© OR PEPTO-BISMAL© TO THE BABY to stop the diarrhea.

Diarrhea is a physiologic response to an irritant or infection in the infant's bowel. The body tries to get rid of the irritation by washing the irritant off with intestinal juices. It is advisable to aid the body by flushing the bowel with clear liquids, e.g., Pedialyte©, or Lytren©. When the irritant disappears, the diarrhea will stop. If your baby's diarrhea persists, other causes for the diarrhea may exist, e.g., infectious diarrhea. Your doctor must determine what caused the parenteral diarrhea and institute measures to correct it as soon as possible.

Another symptom that concerns new parents is constipation. Bottle fed babies commonly develop constipation. This is because the free water content in cow's milk is lower than the free water content in human breast milk. You can easily help your baby resolve the constipation by giving him water between feedings. You may also add one tablespoon of dark Karo© syrup to four ounces of water; boil and cool them together, then feed it to your baby. Do not ever use honey as it may cause infantile botulism. You may also add a teaspoonful of Maltsupex© powder into every ounce of formula. This will keep the bulk in the intestinal lumen and prevent constipation.

Constipation can be dangerous if not relieved by these simple measures. The baby will need to be examined. Please expect your physician to do a rectal examination to find out whether the baby suffers from Hirschsprung's disease, a condition that may require surgical intervention for correction.

Occasionally, breastfed babies also can become constipated and usually no good reason for this can be found. Typically these babies look well, are not irritable, and do not feel distended. The only reasonable explanation for this phenomenon that has been accepted is, since breastmilk is the ideal food for that baby, the baby may digest and absorb every drop of breast milk he takes in, leaving no residue for stools. The infant may go without a bowel movement for up to a week at a time. However, you should let your doctor know so that he or she can monitor your baby's progress and check for any early abnormal signs or symptoms.

Feeding Your Newborn

Human breastmilk is best for human infants. The Nutrition Committee of the American Academy of Pediatrics recommends breastfeeding. Also, experts in infant nutrition have determined that the best nutrients for an infant are in breast milk. However, if you decide that breastfeeding is not for you after due deliberation by both parents, there are acceptable infant formulas to substitute for breastmilk. Any humanized formula is acceptable. Commercially prepared, iron fortified, cow based formulas (Similac©, Enfamil©) are reasonable alternatives. Your pediatrician prefers a milk-based formula over a soy formula in general, particularly during the first month of life. This is because the galactose fraction of the lactose molecule helps glycogen deposition in the liver cells, preventing hypoglycemic attacks between feedings. However, there are specific indications on when to use soy formulas, so please discuss this with your doctor before you decide to change formulas for your infant.

It is not necessary or advisable to start mixed feedings (solids) before four to six months of age. Babies need only breastmilk or formula for the first four to six months of life. Evidence suggests that babies may have difficulty digesting and absorbing solids introduced before that age. Solid food is expensive and may add to overfeeding and obesity. Overfeeding causes more harm than good. Overfeeding will not calm a baby. Over-distending an infant's stomach will cause pain and discomfort for the baby. Obese infants will eventually become obese adults, with all the complications that may go with obesity.

It may be advisable to introduce mixed feeding after four to six months of age. Please start with cereal, then fruit and vegetables, and finally meat and poultry. Always start one new food at a time. Give the new food during the morning feeding and continue offering the new food for at least four to five days before you switch or add another new food. Please do not use mixed cereal when you start introducing cereals. Should your baby develop any symptoms after a mixed cereal, it is difficult to determine which one of the several components caused the symptom or discomfort that your baby may exhibit.

If you use city water for drinking, your doctor may suggest that you use purified water to feed your infant to avoid the unduly high concentration of fluoride in the water that may stain your child's teeth. If you do choose to use purified water, please let your physician know so that he or she may prescribe the appropriate amount of fluoride for your infant to prevent dental cavities.

It is not essential to give additional vitamins to your infant if he is formula-fed. It is, however, okay to give vitamins to him if you choose to do so. Any brand will do. They all provide the essential vitamins in sufficient quantities. For breastfed infants, the customary vitamins are: Vitamin A, Vitamin C, Vitamin D, and fluoride if your baby requires no additional water or if your water is purified.

During the first few weeks of life, you may find that your infant is difficult to satisfy by feeding. Babies wants to eat all the time, particularly when they are awake. As a matter of fact, you may recall that your fetus in utero was fed continuously for nine months. With every contraction of your heart, nutrients were delivered through the placenta to the fetus. Just imagine that you have been snacking all the time for the past nine months and suddenly you are asked to take meals. If you do not know when your next meal would be, you will probably be concerned and tend to stuff yourself. Your newborn infant does the same thing. This is normal. Your infant may stuff himself to the point of spitting up, or the stomach distention may create abdominal cramps. It is not necessary to over-feed your infant. You will not over-feed by nursing your infant. Your breastmilk supply will limit over-feeding. By emptying your breast, you will produce more milk. A hormone produced in your brain regulates breastmilk production. On the other hand, our nation is blessed with an unlimited supply of formula either at the grocery store or via the government's nutritional program. Good intentioned parents and guardians unintentionally over-feed infants, creating health problems for these infants and the current obesity epidemic in our country. Bottle-fed infants should not get more than two and a half ounces of formula per pound of body weight per twenty-four hours. By simply dividing the total quantity of the formula needed by 10 or 12, depending on the number of feedings you intend to provide for your infant, you should get the correct volume of formula to put in each bottle, ready to feed your baby. This volume of full strength formula will provide the nutrition, calories, and fluid your infant needs to grow and develop. Do not over-feed your infant.

The following feeding practices are recommended:
   A) **Birth to 4-6 months**: breastmilk or iron-containing cow milk based formula: no solids, no juices. For every pound of body weight, an infant needs two and a half ounces of formula per twenty-four hours.

   B) **4-6 months:** continue breastmilk or formula; may begin to introduce solids.

   C) **6-12 months:** continue breastmilk or formula; add solids so the child eventually receives cereals, fruits, vegetables, and meats; introduce juices.

Solid Foods

It is probably irrelevant which solid food one introduces first. When asked, your pediatrician usually recommends rice cereal first because rice protein contains all the essential amino acids for protein synthesis. One should begin with a small amount (1 or 2 teaspoons) first thing in the morning, observing the infant for the rest of the day. You want to observe for signs of indigestion, abdominal distention, cramping or diarrhea. The morning introduction of a new food provides you time to observe the infant; otherwise, any intolerance may end up disturbing the baby's rest and your sleep that night. A new food should be given once a day at first. If tolerated, give twice a day, advancing to one or two tablespoons per feeding. Also introduce a spoon when feeding solids. It is a practical rule to introduce only one new food item at a time, feeding it for four or five days before introducing another new food. Thus, if a rash or diarrhea follows as a result of the new food, the offender will be obvious. Infants do not crave a variety (though society seems to view the eating of increasing varieties of food by babies as elevated status), so do not be in a hurry to give too many foods. DO NOT USE AN INFANT FEEDER. Your infant needs to learn to swallow solid food by using his tongue to form a small bolus and swallow the food. Using an infant feeder delays this learning process. This delay may be harmful for your infant.

By six-seven months of age, your infant should be having two or three small "meals" a day of solid foods. By nine-twelve months of age, the infant should be having three meals a day with snacks in between. By one year of age, the formula intake (if bottle-fed) or the number of breastfeedings should have decreased to three or four times in a 24 hour period. By one year of age, the infant should be weaned off the bottle. The nighttime bottle should be the first one to discontinue. The milk residue in the infant's mouth ferments during sleep and may ruin his teeth. After one year of age, the child should receive homogenized whole cow milk at eight ounces or less per 24 hours. Skim milk and 2% milk should not be given to children under the age of two years. Skim milk is acceptable for children over two years of age. You may still want to breastfeed your infant after his first birthday. It should be totally up to you and your family when you wean. You should understand that the longer you breastfeed your baby beyond one year of age, the harder it may be for him to give up nursing. He may embarrass you in public when he wants to be breastfed. He may try to undress you in public when he wants to nurse!

The following recommendations about feeding are useful hints:
1) Do not buy "meat dinners" since they contain more vegetables than meat. Though the meat dinners are cheaper than pure meat, they are

actually more expensive when taking into consideration the amount of meat they contain.

2) Do not introduce egg whites or wheat before nine months of age because they are common allergy inducers.

3) Chocolate and peanut butter are very common allergens and are best avoided in the first two years of life.

4) Children under the age of five have difficulty eating nutty material; they frequently choke on such foods aspirating them into their lungs. Such aspirations may require surgical procedures to remove the material. Do not feed nuts or popcorn before five years of age!

5) Do not give whole hot-dogs to a toddler, he may walk around or run around with it and choke. Hot-dog sausages should be cut into bite size pieces for your toddlers. By six years of age, they should be able to handle a whole hot dog.

Though some may feel the above guidelines are excessive, there are no known requirements for any of the above foods nor are there any deficiency states known in children who have not received them.

Breastfeeding

Assume a position that is comfortable for you and hold the baby so that his tummy is below his head and his tummy is facing your tummy. Gently touch your nipple to the baby's cheek and the baby open wide to grasp the nipple. The baby should nurse with about an inch to an inch and a half of the pigmented part of the breast in his mouth. When you wish to remove the baby from the breast, break the suction by pushing a finger down on your breast at the corner of the baby's mouth. Pulling the baby off your nipple before your break the suction may result in tender, sore nipples.

Wash your nipples when you take a bath using clear water. Soap may dry your nipple area as avoid it on your breasts. Some milk may leak from your breasts between feedings. A cotton nursing pad inside your brassiere will absorb the milk. You may find that supporting your breast with one hand while breastfeeding may be more comfortable than no support at all and will help the baby hold the breast in his mouth.

You may find that when your baby begins nursing on one breast, milk may leak from the other breast. This "let-down reflex" is normal so it should not concern you. Nurse your baby until he "falls off" the first breast. Burp your baby and offer the other breast. Listen for swallowing sounds to make sure your baby is getting milk.

Start with a different breast at each feeding, thereby ensuring that your baby will empty both breasts and thus fully stimulate them to produce milk at least every two feedings. Your baby will want to nurse more frequently at first since a newborn's tummy is very small and breastmilk is quickly digested. The more your baby nurses, the more milk you will produce. A schedule for breastfeeding is not necessary. Try to nurse your infant on demand at least 10 -12 times in a 24 hour period. You can create demand by waking your baby often. Feed your baby when your baby is hungry. Your baby will tell you that he is hungry by sucking on his lips, cheeks, fingers, or fist; rooting; fussing, or crying. Crying is a late hunger cue. Try to nurse your baby when he shows the early hunger cues. Awaken and exercise your baby during the daytime to play and to nurse so that your baby may learns to stay awake during the day and sleep at night.

Some mothers become concerned that their babies are not getting enough breast milk and "to be on the safe side" begin to supplement breast-feeding with formula. If you are concerned about whether or not your baby is getting sufficient breast milk, please contact your doctor and discuss the problems. Your baby is getting enough milk if he wets six-eight very wet dia-pers a day, has at least three substantial (fist full) bowel movements, nurses for longer than five minutes and acts satisfied when he releases the breast, you hear the baby swallowing or see milk running out of his mouth, and he gains weight steadily. Please do not make changes without a discussion with your physician first. Emptying your breast stimulates the production of more breastmilk. On the other hand, supplementation decreases demand and you start to make less milk. A neural hormone regulates breastmilk production through a feedback mechanism.

Another common problem is that your milk supply may not increase as quickly as you want. Most women will not have a good milk supply until the third or the fourth day after delivery. This is normal. The colostrum, the thick first milk, is very good for the baby. Let your baby nurse and stimulate your breast - your milk supply will increase. It takes time for you to get a full milk supply, usually four to six weeks. Be patient with yourself. You will make enough milk for your baby. Drink an adequate amount of fluid, eat enough calories, relax, and nurse often. You will provide six to seven hundred calories to the baby a day. The more you empty your breast, the more milk you will produce. It is all right to pump your breast in the early postpartum period to stimulate your milk flow. Your doctor may also prescribe a nose spray to help you to achieve letdown. Both can be used safely.

Since it is desirable for you to have some free time away from your baby, you can occasionally pump your breasts, putting the breastmilk in a plastic bag or bottle and using it for feeding later. Breastmilk can be stored in a freezer for up to several months at a time. Label your breastmilk with the date and time. Thaw out the earliest one and use them according to chronological order. This will let your baby get used to taking milk from a bottle, thereby allowing you to be able to skip a feeding or two. This will not confuse the baby. Your baby can adapt to your schedule. You may use an electric breast pump or a manual pump. Or, you may find manual expression of breastmilk preferable to using a pump. These techniques can be demonstrated to you if you wish by your doctor or lactation specialist.

Once you establish your milk supply, it will not hurt you or your baby to miss an occasional breastfeeding. In such instances, you may use commercial formula or you may thaw out frozen breastmilk to use on such occasions.

If you have older children, particularly young toddlers between the ages of two to three years old, they may be jealous when the baby is breast-feeding. You can have several sets of toys and books around you when you set up to nurse the baby. Instead of the older siblings dragging you around to do services in order to interrupt the nursing period, you can distract them by asking them to read a book or play with some of the toys. Try to change the topic every minute or two to keep them busy. By receiving your attention, they feel that their mother is still playing with them. It is all right to teach your baby girls to breastfeed their dolls. This will introduce the concept of breastfeeding to them early, teaching them that they should nurse their babies in the future.

How long you breastfeed is up to you. When you decide to stop breastfeeding, your doctor can discuss with you what you are going to use to feed your baby.

If your breasts develop a tenderness or redness that lasts for two or three feedings, contact your doctor, but do not become alarmed. It is common to have plugged ducts in your breast. A hot shower or gentle expression of the firm area usually helps. If this situation persists, inform your doctor.

A book you will find most helpful for breastfeeding and its associated problems is: *The Complete Book of Breastfeeding* by Marvin Eager, M.D. and Sally Wendkos Olds.

Bottle-feeding

The choice of bottle type is rarely critical. The feeding technique used is more important than which bottles or nipples are used. Hold the baby close to you, supporting the head. You should elevate the head so that it is higher than the stomach. Tilt the bottle at an angle so that formula always fills the bottleneck and the nipple. If the nipple becomes collapsed from suction, remove it from the baby's mouth and give the baby a brief rest. At the same time, loosen the cap of the bottle a little, so that air can enter the bottle as the baby consumes the formula. Never prop the bottle or feed the baby while the baby is lying flat. Doing so greatly enhances the possibility of choking and aspirating milk into the lungs, resulting in pneumonia. Also, such practices have been associated with a higher incidence of ear infections.

As previously stated, most of the iron-containing, milk-based commercially prepared formulas are acceptable. Some commonly used formula are Similac© and Enfamil©. If milk allergy is a problem in your family, let your doctor know. A non-milk based formula might be preferable for your baby, particularly after the crucial period of the first four to six weeks of life.

Feed your baby on demand, feeding him when he is hungry. Burp the baby two or three times during each feeding. Some infants feed more slowly than others, so it should not alarm you if your baby feeds slower or faster than other babies. Enlarging the holes in the nipple or using a cross-cut nipple to increase the speed with which the infant feeds may result in choking or aspiration. Nipples do occasionally become clogged and require unplugging, but you should not enlarge the hole unless they are abnormally small.

You should sterilize your bottles and formula. Two different methods are described below. Your doctor may recommend sterilization of bottles and formula for the first four months of the baby's life. After the first four months, your baby's gastrointestinal immunity may be mature enough that dish-washer cleaning with extra rinsing is sufficient.

Terminal Sterilization
1) Wash bottles and nipples and prepare formula according to directions on the can of formula.

2) Fill bottles with formula, place sealing cap into bottle cap, turn nipple up side down and place cap on bottle loosely (so that the nipple is sticking down into the formula.)

3) Place the bottles in a pan or sterilizer and use a rack or cloth under the bottles to cushion.

4) Put 3-4 inches of water in pan or sterilizer. Cover pan and boil gently for 25 minutes.

5) Remove pan from heat and allow to cool.

6) Tighten caps on bottles, then refrigerate until used.

Separate Sterilization of Bottles and Formula

1) Wash bottles, nipples, caps, and any utensils necessary for pouring formula into bottles (i.e. funnel, punch type can opener.)

2) Rinse thoroughly, forcing water through nipple holes to be certain they are clear.

3) Place all of the above in a pan or sterilizer and use a cloth under bottles to cushion.

4) Put 3-4 inches of water in the pan or sterilizer, cover pan, and boil the contents for 15 minutes.

5) Remove pan from heat and allow to cool (leave lid on pan while cooling.)

6) When bottles are cool enough to handle, you may choose to fill them one at a time at the time for each feeding or all at once. If you fill all the bottles at one time, cap them, and store them in the refrigerator.

Preparation of Formula

Preparation will depend on the method of sterilization used and whether you are using ready-to-feed formula or liquid concentrate. One form is as good as the other. The cost, however, is not identical. The most expensive is the most convenient (ready-to-feed formula). The least expensive is the least convenient (powder formula).

With terminal sterilization, everything is sterilized at once as the last step after contact with all utensils used. If bottles are sterilized separately, then all utensils used (pitchers, spoons, can openers) must be sterilized and any water used for dilution must first be boiled.

Ready-to-Feed Formula

Pour boiling water over top of can and use a sterilized can opener to open the can. Formula is ready to be used as is. Simply pour the formula into a pre-sterilized bottle, seal them lightly, and the bottle is ready to feed to your baby. You should store the remaining formula in pre-sterilized bottles, seal them, and put them into the refrigerator for later use. Avoid freezing them.

Liquid Concentrate Formula

Follow dilution instructions on the can. Mix formula with sterilized water either in each bottle or in a sterilized pitcher, and then pour into bottles for storage.

Powder Formula

Follow dilution instructions on the can. Mix separately in each bottle or all at once in a sterilized pitcher and then pour into bottles for later use. Be cautious of over diluting powdered formula- you may not be delivering enough calories and nutrition to your infant. Avoid putting in too much formula powder and making the bottle too concentrated. Your infant may not get enough free water and this may be hazardous to your infant.

It is apparent that breastfeeding an infant is the preferred, convenient method of providing nutrition to your newborn. Mothers should seriously consider breastfeeding their infants. The American Academy of Pediatrics recommends breastfeeding at least through the first year of your infant's life. Breastfeeding is a big commitment that will benefit both you and your baby!

Well Child Check-up Visits

Pediatricians believe in periodic well child visits. These visits occur more often in the first two years. After that, children should have yearly physical examinations to record their growth and developmental parameters. There are specific goals for each well check examination. Your physician may want to draw your attention to any special problems during this period of growth and development. The examination also serves as a way to increase communication between you, your child, and your pediatrician. Usually during a sick visit, you are so concerned about your sick child (which is normal) that it is impossible for your doctor to tell you how to manage anything else except that particular illness. As children grow, they go through periods of adjustment and adaptation to their environment. They need your guidance. It is the duty of your pediatrician to help you develop guidelines for your children appropriate to their stage of development. Just like the regular maintenance work on your car, a brake job does not necessarily include an oil change or even tightening the various belts on the engine. Well visits for your youngster are just like the routine maintenance on your automobile: they serve a different purpose for each individual visit.

The well child schedules are based on the recommendation of the American Academy of Pediatrics as follows:

10 days to 2 weeks	1 year
2 months	15 months
4 months	18 months
6 months	2 years
9 months	Yearly thereafter

However, with the recent trend of early hospital discharge of postpartum mothers and newborns, many pediatricians request that you to bring your infant to the office earlier than ten days to two weeks, to have a quick follow-up on neonatal jaundice, feeding issues, and to provide more teaching than you were able to receive during your hospital stay.

Your doctor will expect your child to receive immunizations. It is through immunizations that we have been able to control some infectious diseases and eradicate smallpox. You can get immunizations at the local Health

Department (for a small fee) or at your doctor's office. Your doctor has to charge for the immunization because he or she has to buy the vaccines from the manufacturers. In most states, you are required to have your children immunized before they are registered for school. The immunization schedule changes periodically. (See Appendix A.) Thus, it is prudent to consult your doctor about appropriate immunizations during well child visits.

Typically, anticipatory guidance topics are also scheduled during the well child visits. It is important for you to formulate questions and prepare for discussions about your child's health and well-being in these sessions. Some doctors use group sessions. If you are unable or unwilling to have an open discussion in a group setting, please let your doctor know so that special arrangements can be made to accommodate your situation. Some pediatricians may use nurse practitioners to help them to do well child care. They are trained professionals and qualified providers of well child care and care for simple, routine, and common illnesses . If care is provided by the nurse practitioner, you should still be able to discuss any concerns you have with your doctor if you prefer. It is your choice.

part

The Two-Week-Old

Now that you have a true taste of parenthood. You may feel tired all the time, maybe even more tired than during your pregnancy. You lack sleep and are up most of the night with a crying, fussing infant. Unfortunately, you cannot trade him in for a new model. This is a commitment for life. Do not be scared by your crying, fussing infant. Crying and fussing will not hurt him. Crying and fussing are his only communication skills at this point. They carry some messages. Try to learn the meaning of his communication and his messages. Accept your baby. Teach him your preferred communication skills. It is your desire to have children. It is not your infant's fault. You will have fun soon.

By now, you should feel comfortable with your infant. You should have a list of questions for your doctor when you come in for your two week check-up: the things that you are not sure of, the little movements your infant makes, the funny noises, the peeling skin etc. You should write them down before the checkup so you can remember to ask your doctor. Most doctors already have a fair idea of what you are wondering about. They may address them during the checkup session. However, if your doctor does not do that, it is your responsibility to ask them specifically so that your queries and your concerns are answered.

Ideally, your physician's office staff has already collected all the demographic data from you. This can facilitate your first visit to the doctor's office. Most of the delivery history should already be in the folder. The office nurse will weigh your infant and measure your infant's length and head circumference.

59

The record should include the birth weight and length. Do not be surprised that your baby shrank in the two week period. This is because of the molding of the head that your infant had during the birth process. Now that the molding has subsided, the measurement should be the true length of your infant. However, measuring the infant is notoriously inaccurate since an infant will not obey orders to hold still. Yet, it is important to record these parameters because they will be plotted on a growth curve to compare your infant with the national average. These measurements are used to establish a trend on the growth curve for your baby. (See Appendix B.) Most babies should regain the weight that was lost after birth by two weeks of age and start to gain about an ounce a day.

Your doctor will come in at this point and start the visit. This normally begins with a brief greeting and questions about how you have been doing for the past two weeks. The history taking by your doctor should include feeding, assessment of the infant's development, the physical examination, and a brief discussion of the problems and the plan of action for the next six weeks or so until the next visit at the two-month checkup.

The maternal history should include the general well being of the mother. This is a period of "postpartum blues" when the new mother may be depressed about the whole issue of parenthood. This is normal and your doctor should be sensitive about it and help you to find help and support. Family support is normally the best way to go, followed by friends and church groups. Sometimes, social agencies may help find ways to solve problems that are unforeseeable. Do not hesitate to get help. This stage will pass with time. If it becomes severe, psychiatric evaluation may be necessary with the appropriate intervention and rehabilitative measures planned.

A nutritional history will include the method, frequency, and the amount of feeding. This is further evaluated by the rate of the infant's weight gain, the number of wet diapers, and the frequency of bowel movements. As indicated above, the infant should gain back the weight-loss from the first week of life, have six to eight wet diapers per twenty-four hour period, and have at least one or two good bowel movements a day. This may vary from infant to infant. Your doctor will be making the assessment of your infant during the physical examination.

A certain amount of developmental screening is usually carried out during the visit. Most of them are observational, and your doctor performs some of them. Your physician may ask you questions about what you have observed at home when the infant is asleep or when you are holding and caring for the baby, or he or she may make direct observations during the physical examination. There is a wide range of normalcy; your infant's performance may not necessarily raise concern. By and large, a two-week-old infant is able to turn his head from side to side and to fixate on an object, particularly the mother's face or light in the line of vision. When your infant tries to focus, it is not unusual to find him crossing his eyes. This is because most infants are far-sighted and it is difficult for him to focus on a near object. The infant sees clearest at about twelve inches from the object. Your baby should be able to respond to a loud noise with the normal startle reflex. Hearing screens on newborn infants are carried out by most hospitals in the United States. The results of your infant's hearing screen should be available at this time. Your baby should hear normally.

The physical examination should be comprehensive. Expect your doctor/nurse practitioner to undress the baby completely. Your doctor may point out some observations that he or she makes about your infant, such as the healing of the fetal monitoring electrode wound on the scalp. The bruising of the forceps marks should be gone by now, yet the cephalhematoma may still be there. This is normal and should not cause any concern. Baby acne may be apparent. This normally subsides gradually within the next few weeks. You can use a hydrogen peroxide solution diluted with water to wash the area. This will suffice. If there is a lot of redness on the skin, cellulitis may have already developed. You should let your doctor know and see if your infant needs to be examined in the office.

By state law, most areas in the United States require putting chemicals into the baby's eye for prophylaxis against eye infections. You may find that your baby's eye has a discharge. It may be clear or purulent. This normally subsides in a matter of days; however, if it persists there may be a problem. If your baby's eye is still weeping by two weeks of age, it usually indicates that the tear duct on that side is blocked or narrowed. Typically, tears run out of the eye onto the cheek on that side . You can gently massage the tear duct with the tip of your little finger every time you feed your baby. This will help to prevent infection and help to force the tear duct open. This tear duct problem may last for up to nine months to a year. Unfortunately, if it persists much longer than a year, your doctor will normally refer you to an ophthalmologist to surgically irrigate or probe the tear duct open.

The frenulum is a fold of tissue extending from the floor of the mouth to the bottom of the tongue. Sometimes, it is tight. As long as your baby can move his tongue and has no problems eating, you do not need to worry about a tight frenulum. Clipping the frenulum is not necessary most of the time. However, the tongue should be examined with respect to the chin. A protruding tongue may indicate problems like hypothyroidism, mongolism, or other chromosomal problems or different syndromes. A mass on top of the tongue may indicate a misplaced thyroid gland. Surgically removing it without due consideration is not prudent. Gum buds are common. Some babies may even have neonatal teeth. Those need to be taken care of by a pediatric dentist. Oral thrush may appear as early as two weeks of age. Thrush is a fungus which appears as milk-curd-like patches on the inside cheek of the mouth. When you wipe them, they leave a raw surface and may bleed. This is a yeast infection of the mouth. You may need to inform your doctor and see if he or she would like to examine your infant, or they may provide advice on medication for your infant and give you specific instructions on how to take care of it. If you are breastfeeding your infant when he develops thrush, you may need topical treatment on your nipples.

By two weeks of age, your baby should be able to move his neck symmetrically. Sometimes, however, this is not the case. Your baby may have congenital torticollis. In general, this is not a major concern. It develops because the neck muscles are stretched during the delivery process. Your doctor may teach you how to manipulate the baby's neck to exercise it. This will soon be better with time. Sometimes, your doctor may refer you to a physical therapist who may teach you the exercise techniques and supervise your exercise program. True congenital developmental abnormalities of the cervical spine are so obvious at birth that you will notice them before your baby is discharged from the hospital.

At times, a lump is found on the baby's neck. This may be a small hematoma on the sternomastoid muscle, and it will resolve in due time. It is typically associated with the torticollis described above. Sometimes, you may feel a knot on the collarbone. This is of no concern, also. It happened during the delivery process when the collarbone was being compressed, bruised, or fractured. Normally, it will heal by itself without any intervention. If you notice it, you may want to handle your baby's shoulder on the affected side carefully because moving the shoulder may be painful for the baby. Another knot that may concern you is one on the tip of the wishbone. It is noticeable at the mid-chest. It is pointed and should not cause any problem. As soon as the baby develops some muscle and fat, it will be covered. Sometimes a dimple is noticeable in the mid-sternum. It is an inherited condition called pectus excavatum or funnel-chest. It is rather benign and does not require excessive attention. Again, when the musculature of the chest wall starts to develop, it will look better. It normally does not require surgical intervention.

Movements of the infant will be observed with particular reference to joint movements. Spreading of the legs (abduction) is performed to detect any dislocation of the hips. Flexion and extension of the elbow and knees are done to demonstrate to the parents that the extremities of the infant are not straight. This will emphasize to them that they need to exercise the infant. Similarly, movements of the feet, ankles and heel cords will be performed. Some infants have "club-foot" caused by their in-utero positioning. Positional club-foot can be corrected by exercise alone. Structural "club-foot" may require orthopedic attention. To some degree, the stiffness of the infant's joints is normal because of the in-utero positioning; however, excessive stiffness may mean arthrogyposis, a condition that needs medical attention and appropriate physical therapy with many follow-up visits.

Your pediatrician will proceed with the rest of the physical examination. Listening to the chest (auscultation) will find normal breath sounds and normal heart sounds. However, it is not uncommon to pick up abnormal heart sounds and heart murmurs at the two-week visit. This is due to the physiological changes of the heart around the time of birth (the ductus arteriosus and the Foramen of Ovale need to be closed). The drop of the pulmonary arterial pressure may provide a gradient for a shunt to develop if there is an abnormal left to right shunt. As long as the infant is asymptomatic and not in congestive heart failure, one can safely observe the infant for further development of the cardiovascular status. The abdomen will be palpated for any enlargement of the organs. The liver, spleen, and kidneys may be palpated. The umbilical cord stump will be examined for possible infection, granulation, or other abnormal discharge. Some infants may still carry the cord stump. This needs to be noted because prolonged separation of the cord may mean a functional white blood cell defect in the infant. If there is an umbilical nodule, expect your doctor to use a silver nitrate stick to paint on the granulation tissue. This will hasten the healing of the navel.

Particularly for a breastfeeding infant, one may still detect some jaundice. Breastmilk jaundice has not been shown to be harmful to the infant. One should not be alarmed by it. Yet, it is prudent to follow the degree of jaundice until its final disappearance. Indirect sun-bathing of the infant may be helpful to hasten the recovery process. The conjugation process of the bilirubin may be delayed by breastfeeding. Usually by the fourth month, breastmilk jaundice should disappear completely. If elevated bilirubin persists, one should suspect inborn-errors of metabolism involving bilirubin transport and conjugation.

The primitive reflexes may still be present at this time, and your doctor may want to demonstrate them. The startle reflex, the stepping reflex, and the grasp reflexes of the hands and feet are all normal, so are some of the twitching and jerking movements of the infant. Remember, if you have any questions during the physical examination, please do not hesitate to ask your doctor.

If you have other children, expect your doctor to ask about them and their reaction to the new baby. Sibling rivalry is normal. Depending on the ages of your other children, they will react differently. A clinical psychologist once used this example: a husband brings home another woman, telling his wife that she is just another wife. He expects his first wife to accept her, be nice to her, and work with her. You would, of course, expect the first wife to be angry, resentful, and upset about the whole thing. Basically, when you brought the newborn home from the hospital, you have created the same type of problem for your other children. This is particularly true if the older sibling is still fairly young (less than three years of age), unable to comprehend the reasoning, difficult to reason with or be reassured.

Encouraging your older children to get involved in caring for the newborn is a good strategy against the feelings of jealousy. Before you feed your newborn, spread out toys and books for your older ones to play with while you are holding and feeding the baby. Get several toys and books. Your older child will think that the twenty minutes or so of nursing time is forever. So, read a story to them, have several toys around and play with them, and then they should not be dragging you around to do this or that to disrupt the nursing. Of course, if you have older children, involve them in caring for the new baby. They will share the joy of having a new member in the family. Talk to your teenage daughter, in particular, about the responsibilities of being a parent. She may think that having a baby is so much fun that she may want to have her own child!

You will also find that there are a lot of well wishers. Accept their generosity and well wishing. It is all right to let them know that you may not need a thousand receiving blankets or newborn outfits. Set up an account for your newborn and request that they give cash to be put into the account for future use. It is not too early to start a college tuition fund for your newborn.

Now that the new baby has come, it is also time to look at your life insurance policy. You need to make provisions for the support of this youngster if something happens to you or your spouse. You can obtain inexpensive term life insurance; or better still, you can use universal life policies as your saving plan. These will serve the purpose of insurance as well. If you are financially sophisticated, you may consider buying a life insurance policy for your baby.

If you prepare a long list of questions for this visit, let your doctor know ahead of time so that the time for your visit can be adjusted. Most offices allot a specific amount of time for each visit. If you let your doctor know, he can allow more time for the visit. If you tie up the doctor for too long, you may face some ugly looks from other patients when you leave the office. Obviously, the receptionist is there to serve you. But, she is also the one to answer to the other waiting patients while you are visiting with the doctor. You do want to develop a good, working relationship with her. This will make your time in the doctor's office easier in the future.

The Two-Month-Old

By two months of age, most infants learn to sleep all night. Thank goodness. Yet, you may remember the first time your baby slept through the night and you awoke frightened that you did not hear your baby cry. You rushed into the baby's room to see if every parent's nightmare had happened to you (your baby died of sudden infant death syndrome) only to find that your little sweetheart was still sound asleep, breathing nicely and easily. You sat down greatly relieved. This is parenthood. You will find that you are in an anxiety state most of the time, making decisions about your baby's life, and wondering whether you are doing the right thing or not. It is scary.

The two-month check-up is normally a happy one. After the office nurse weighs and measures your naked baby, you cover the baby with a receiving blanket, change the diaper if necessary, and wait for the doctor to come. In the mean time, you can console your infant if the nurse disrupted his sleep or snack. You can also start making a list of questions to ask the doctor if you have not already done so.

As the doctor greets you with a smile, asking you how things are at home, your visit begins. Your pediatrician normally asks questions about your infant. How much he is eating? How is his sleeping pattern? Do the infant's eyes follow you past midline? Does the baby smile socially or coo? Does the baby roll around yet? This may go on for five to ten minutes, with one question after another. At the same time, your doctor writes down your answers, making notes on the baby's chart. Time and again, your doctor may ask you how you feel about your infant. This is important because your pediatrician needs to know exactly how you feel before giving appropriate advice.

With the measured weight and length, your doctor may plot your baby's weight and length on a growth chart, indicating to you how your baby compares with the "average" baby in the United States of America. This is an "assumed" normal growth curve. However, it does not take into consideration your background, your ethnicity, habits, altitude where you reside, and the season of the year. All these things may affect the growth of your baby. Let your doctor make the interpretation.

Moreover, it is the trend of growth that is important, rather than the isolated data on a particular visit. Commonly, during the first weeks of life, the baby gains about an ounce per day. This will slow down as time goes on. Do not worry about the weight alone.

The head circumference is another important measurement for an infant. This is also plotted on the growth curve. An enlarged head is not good and may signify a problem. In the case of an enlarged head, there may be more in the head than just the brain. Hydrocephalus is not uncommon. This may not be present at birth, but may show up at this age. Fortunately, this can be corrected surgically by putting in a shunt, and the infant may progress normally. An abnormally small head is not good, either. This is usually more of a problem than a big head. If the sutures in the skull closed prematurely (synostosis), this may stop brain growth, increasing the pressure inside the infant's head, and causing symptoms. If the brain inside the skull is not growing, the head will not grow either. Microcephaly has many causes. Your doctor needs to determine the etiology of microcephaly. On the other hand, synostosis is also an operable condition. With the proper neurosurgical procedure, normal brain growth may be restored and normal neuro-development achieved.

The physical examination is performed in a systematic fashion. Your pediatrician starts with the head, eyes, ears, nose and throat and moves on. The tear ducts are checked, the nares inspected, the ear canal and tympanic membranes are examined, followed by the mouth, buccal mucosa, and the throat. It is not unusual to see some signs of teething now. This is considered normal. The tongue and the buccal mucosa are inspected for oral candidiasis (thrush). The gag reflex and the development of the tonsillar tissue are assessed. The tonsils are absent at birth. They develop with time and maturity. They may vary in size. At two months of age, they may barely be noticeable. The complete absence of the tonsillar tissue may indicate immunoincompetence. It may deserve further workup or, at least, be documented on the medical record for future reference. The heart and lungs are auscultated, the abdomen palpated for enlargement of the organs, and all the peripheral pulses are checked. The hips are abducted and checked for hip clicks. The external genitalia are inspected. In boys, it is crucial to check for the descent of the testis, and in girls, for the adhesion of the labia. Undescended testis at this stage should not cause a big concern. The right time to correct it is between nine months to a year of age. However, it needs to be followed carefully and must be well documented on the medical record. Labial adhesion is very common in baby girls. The infant girl does not secrete enough female hormones (estrogen) at this age causing the adhesion. Some doctors prefer to separate it manually; however, most commonly, your pediatrician may prescribe an estrogen cream to apply to the adhesion area. The estrogen vaginal cream comes with an applicator for an adult woman. The applicator may do more harm than good to the labial adhesion. Your doctor may recommend obtaining a new watercolor brush. Wash it, dip it into the cream, and paint it onto the area of the adhesion. Usually, it takes a couple of weeks to open the adhesion. This should not be of great concern. Using too much of the vaginal cream may provide an excessive amount of estrogen that may cause harm. This may cause other hormone-sensitive tissue to develop. Remember, when you stop using the cream, the labial adhesion may recur because your little girl may not produce an adequate amount of estrogen until she enters puberty. Check your baby girl's genitalia often for this condition, particularly when she is out of the diaper age.

Eczema is a scaly, crusting skin lesion that is common at this age. It can usually be found behind the ears, on the face, and around the chin. A small amount of steroid cream will take care of it. It should cause no concern. However, it may signal allergies. One needs to be careful when introducing new chemicals - from lotions, detergents, creams, or food later on. Breastfed infants may also have eczema. Excessive amounts of eczema, together with frequent ear infections and petechiae, may indicate a serious condition called Wiskott - Aldrich syndrome. This may signify an immune defect on the T-lymphocyte system. The infant needs an immunological work-up as soon as possible to protect him from recurrent infection and decrease the chances of immunological reconstitute.

Cradle cap (seborrhea) is also common. One can use a soft brush to comb the hair or use a medicated shampoo like Neutrogena T-gel™ or Selsum Blue™ shampoo. This will normally take care of the problem.

Typically, the two-month-old infant is very susceptible to infection. This is because the transplacental immunity from the mother is gone by now, and the natural postnatal immunity is just beginning to develop. If you are breastfeeding your infant, you are giving the infant secretory IGA and macrophages through the breastfeeding. Yet still, this is not absolute. Your baby can get sick very easily. Do not unnecessarily expose your two-month-old infant to various situations that may increase the risk of infections. This includes church gatherings, large crowds of people, shopping malls, and large family gatherings. Friends, relatives, and children who want to handle your infant need to be reminded to wash their hands and avoid coughing or sneezing on the infant. Avoid cigarette smoke by any means. If the grandparents are smokers, make sure that they change their clothes and wash their hands and face before they hold the baby. At the same time, try to convince them that passive smoking by the baby will increase the baby's risk of respiratory tract infections or sudden death.

This is also the time for the first set of immunizations. It is timed so that it coincides with the lowest immune status of the infant. This facilitates the development of the desired immunity. DTaP (Diphtheria, Tetanus, and acellular Pertussis) Hemophilus Influenza B conjugated vaccine, Pneumococcal conjugated vaccine, Hepatitis B vaccine, and intramuscular Poliomyelitis vaccines are all given at the same time. It has been demonstrated that all these vaccines can be co-administered without interfering with one another. Some parents may think that this is too much for the infant. On the contrary, it is good for the infant to develop immunity as soon as possible and to be immune from these dreadful diseases. It is customary to give the infant acetaminophen to ease the pain and to relieve the expected elevation of body temperature. The usual dosage of acetaminophen should be around 10-15 mg/kg/dose (5mg/lb/dose) given at three to four hour intervals. Some infants may still run a temperature. You can safely use acetaminophen for thirty-six hours or so after the immunization shots. Some infants may cry excessively or have a febrile seizure. Always let your doctor know about any reactions your baby has so that he or she may provide appropriate advice and register the reaction on your baby's record.

Some parents are concerned about vaccinations. This concern is appropriate because you love your children. It is true that vaccinations carry a certain risk because you are introducing a set of stimuli into the youngster's immune system. There are sometimes complications with immunizations. However, the risk/benefit ratio clearly points to the benefit of the vaccinations. One can borrow the example of driving an automobile on the highway. Car accidents claim most young lives in America today. However, no one would ever suggest that you stop driving a car. Only one year of highway mortality/morbidity would well exceed the total known morbidity/mortality caused by all the vaccinations combined since vaccines were introduced to mankind! Nobody has yet met a person who refused to ride in an automobile and went back to walking because of the risk involved with car accidents!

Moreover, there are risks of developing the diseases if one is not protected by vaccination. Pertussis is still in every community because the adult population is a carrier for this infection. Pertussis kills, particularly young infants. The survivor may also be permanently damaged. He may be neurologically affected or have long-term pulmonary damage. Diphtheria may affect the heart or the nervous system. Tetanus in the newborn period also kills, and it is a very painful death. If one were to ever observe a conscious infant with the uncontrollable convulsions of a tetanus victim, one would certainly choose vaccination any time. Ten to fifteen percent of poliomyelitis victims result in permanent paralysis. Hemophilus influenza meningitis kills also, with the lucky survivor suffering from hearing loss, mental retardation, and other long-term effects. Pneumococcal vaccines prevent the invasive form of pneumococcal bacterial infection that cause septicemia, pneumonia, and meningitis. Hepatitis B infection may be silent, only to surface decades later as liver cancer. Vaccination is probably the best buy for your health care dollars. Protect your loved ones by vaccination. For further details on the advantages of vaccines, please visit the website of the Centers of Diseases Control and Prevention at http//: www.cdc.gov. (See Appendix A.)

As you may have already noticed, your infant moves quite readily. Be prepared. Your baby may roll over at any time now. Be aware of the edges of your bed, your changing table, couch, etc. Probably the safest place for a rolling infant is on the floor! Similarly, please do not place your infant carrier/infant seat on anything but the floor because your infant may arch up at any time and dive down. Try not to hold your infant and drink hot drinks, your youngster may grasp the drink burning him and you.

Talk to your infant. Your infant needs to be talked to so that he will develop language skills. He needs to listen to voices and people speaking for about ten months before he starts talking. Try not to talk baby talk. It is normal talking that stimulates the infant. Cooing to the infant will not teach the infant to talk. If you desire to teach your infant a second language, this is a good time to do so. You can imprint up to five or six languages at this age without confusing your infant. Youngsters who grow up in Western Europe typically speak several languages without much of a problem. You may want to tune in the Spanish channels in the southwestern United States or the French channels in Canada to give your infant an added advantage in life.

Tune in some classical music as well. It improves your youngster's mathematical skills! The cortex of the brain that encodes classical music correlates with abstract mathematical concepts. It has been observed that infants brought up in homes that enjoy classical music are good at mathematics later in their lives.

If you are bottle-feeding your infant, you may want to choose a formula that is fortified with iron. By now, your infant may have already out-grown the iron stored in the bone marrow. Typically, by two months of age, iron-fortified formula will no longer irritate your infant's gastro-intestinal tract. In addition, your infant needs the iron for making such things as the hemoglobin in the red blood cells to prevent nutritional anemia and the myoglobin in the muscles. If your baby does not gain a lot of weight, it may be reasonable to wait until four months of age to add the supplemental iron to the formula feeding. This depends on the individual infant.

Similarly, if you are breastfeeding your infant, you should continue your prenatal vitamins and calcium. However, your doctor will supplement your infant with a multiple vitamin with iron and fluoride. This is because vitamins A, C, D, fluoride, and iron do not pass through the breastmilk to the infant. You should continue to eat a healthy diet with plenty of fluid. You may notice that you lose a lot of weight, the weight that you may have gained during your pregnancy. This is normal. It is because you are losing 600-900 calories to your baby every day. Unless you take extra precautions to prevent this weight loss, it is inevitable. However, soon you will compensate by taking in extra calories to accommodate for this calculated loss. Be aware that once you try to wean your infant from breastfeeding (most working mothers will go back to work by two months postpartum), you may need to cut down your calorie intake. Otherwise, you may balloon and gain an excessive amount of weight which may be harmful to your long-term health.

In closing, your doctor may summarize the findings of this check-up by asking you if you have any further questions. He or she will ask you to make another appointment for the four month check-up visit and stress to you that you should not hesitate to call the office for other instructions if you have any problems.

The Four-Month-Old

By the time infants reach four months of age, most working mothers have returned to work. It may be hectic to juggle one's schedule between work, baby-sitting, doctor's appointment and the rest. Be sure to let the receptionist know your schedule so she can make it less stressful for you. Most pediatric offices have morning schedules for well checks and re-checks and reserve the afternoon for sick visits. However, some offices do make exceptions. Some offices have late afternoon well-check schedules, making it more convenient for the working mother. The disadvantage of late afternoon appointments is that the office may be filled with whatever viruses or germs the season brings. It is based on the office receptionist's preference to set the normal well-check schedule.

Again, the office staff will greet you. She may instruct you to go into an examination room and completely undress your infant. The office nurse will then come to weigh and measure your infant, including taking the head circumference. She may ask questions about the feeding, the reactions to the first immunization shots, and any comments you may have before the doctor comes in to start the four month check-up. If you are afraid that your infant may be cold, cover the infant with a receiving blanket and put on the diaper. A few minutes wait is normal, so the baby can be settled down after the measurement and disturbance.

As the physician walks in and greets you, you will find that he or she will have a number of questions for you. Typically, your doctor will start with general questions about you and your family, particularly if you have other children. Then he/she may proceed to ask about the feedings, be it bottle-feeding or breastfeeding. By four months of age, if your infant is bottle-fed, your doctor may tell you that it is no longer necessary to sterilize the bottles or the nipples anymore. Keeping them dishwasher clean may suffice. This is because, by now, your infant has already started to explore the world. Babies can hardly keep their hands off anything that exists around them. Typically, they will put everything that they grasp into their mouths. It is impossible for any parent to sterilize the world. And, by now, the infant has already started to manufacture some immunity to fight the normal germs that he may encounter.

If you are breastfeeding your infant, your doctor may chat with you about the nursing procedure, asking whether you are experiencing any problems. It is uncommon to have breast engorgement or insufficient milk supply at this point because, by now, most likely, you and your infant have worked out the schedule of breastfeeding. Some mothers complain that their infants do not leave them alone, demanding to be nursed all the time. You can introduce a pacifier or a bottle containing breastmilk for your infant. You will not confuse your infant. Your infant will always prefer breastfeeding when it is available. Train your infant. Please do not let your infant control you!

Your doctor may take this opportunity to discuss the introduction of solid food. Routinely, one starts feeding solid food around four to six months of age. It is customary to start with cereals, typically rice powder cereal. By mixing a tablespoon of rice cereal powder with either your breastmilk or formula, you can make a paste and feed the infant with a spoon. Other than the starch content, the rice protein is a complete protein containing all the essential amino acids the infant needs for protein synthesis. It is also fairly hypoallergenic.

It is advisable to introduce solid food early in the morning as the youngster awakens since this is the time that he is most hungry and may accept whatever you offer. Besides, if your infant reacts to the solid, you will have a full day to work with your youngster instead of being kept up all night with the baby crying because of indigestion or abdominal pain. When your infant tolerates the first few feedings of solid food, you may increase both the quantity and the frequency of solid feeding. After the solid feeding, nurse the infant or offer a bottle of formula. Do not be surprised if your infant does not want to consume as much breastmilk or formula; after all, the infant has just finished some food. In between feedings, you may want to breastfeed or bottle-feed your baby. At four months of age, most infants eat seven or eight times a day. Do not use mixed grain cereal. If your infant has a reaction to any one of the components, it is difficult to find out which component your infant does not tolerate. Following cereal introduction, it is customary to introduce fruits, normally white fruits first, like apples, pears, or bananas. Avoid oranges, other citrus fruits, and strawberries at this stage. They are more allergenic than white fruits. When your infant tolerates fruit, you may introduce fruit juices. Then, you may introduce yellow vegetables followed by green vegetables. By six months of age, you may start meat - lean, white meats first, then red meat. There is no definite logic to this way of introduction. However, trial and error shows it to be an efficient way of introducing foods.

Your doctor will then proceed with the rest of the visit. From the measurements that the nursing staff obtained, your doctor may comment on the physical growth of your baby. Remember, it is the trend of growth that is important. As long as the measurements fall on the normal growth curve, one need not be too concerned. Some babies may fall outside the ninety-fifth percentile for weight and/or height, but it does not mean they need to be on a diet. It tells the doctor that they may need to review how you are feeding the baby.

If you are bottle-feeding, it may mean that you are over-feeding the baby. You may need to adjust the volume or the frequency of feeding. However, if you are breastfeeding, you do not need to be alarmed. It has never been shown that a breastfed baby can be overfed. Since the breastmilk supply is based on demand, your baby may just be from large stock. You do not need to cut back on your breastfeeding. Soon, you will find that your four-month-old little darling will not gain weight as fast and will start to slim down. Soon, he will be easily distracted by his surroundings. This may interrupt his consumption of the hind-milk which is high in fat content and calories. His rate of growth will begin to slow down.

By four months, we expect your baby to roll around, start to grasp things that are within reach, giggle, and laugh out loud. He can probably maintain a symmetrical posture most of the time with his head steadied in a sitting position. He may even want to stand up on your lap or on other surfaces with your support. He plays with his hands a lot, looking at them, scratching, and clutching. His arms may activate at the sight of any object, particularly moving ones. His eyes may follow you around. When lying down, he may roll, arch his back, and lift his head at or beyond ninety degrees. A four-month-old infant is usually very sociable. He smiles spontaneously and invites people to play with him. When feeding time comes, he shows his excitement with anticipation.

Because of all the characteristics of a four-month-old infant, caregivers need to be prepared. Responsible baby-sitting is important. Never leave an infant at this age alone on any surface other than the floor, the playpen, or the crib. Infants can roll off the couch or bed in the blink of an eye. When you sit the baby in a high-chair, please remember to buckle the seat-belt. When food is coming, the anticipating infant may pull and grasp for it, not knowing the danger of a fall from the high chair.

Hot objects, be it hot coffee, tea, a curling iron, or a frying pan, should not be left within reach of the baby. Cooking dinner with one hand and holding the baby with the other hand is a dangerous situation that invites an accident. This practice needs to be avoided at all times.

Small particles that the infant may grasp and put into his mouth should not be within reach. Popcorn, nuts, and other small food items can choke an infant at this age. Mother's earrings are a special temptation. Babies love to grasp and pull on these. If you are not prepared for this, you may be startled and in protecting your ears, let your youngster fall. You can easily avoid the situation by not wearing earrings at all or by using stud earrings.

Never prop a bottle. Never leave an infant in bed with a bottle. Always hold him in a reclining position (at least a 45° angle) to feed. This will avoid positional otitis media and rotten teeth.

After giving such advice, your physician may then proceed to the physical examination. Usually, your pediatrician will perform a comprehensive examination, literally from head to toe. A four-month-old will usually allow you to examine him on the examination table. Your doctor usually starts with hip abduction to check for congenital dislocation of the hips. At the same time, he/she checks the femoral pulses, feeling for character, tone and equality on both sides. Before putting the diaper back on, he/she examines the testes in baby boys and looks for labial adhesion in baby girls, simultaneously checking for diaper rash.

He/she then proceeds to examine the scalp for seborrheic dermatitis, the ears for eczema, the eyes, the tear ducts, the ear canals, and the eardrums. He/she checks the mouth for thrush and looks for the development of the tonsillar tissues. Teething may start at this age, and proper oral hygiene needs to be a daily routine. Teething rings and local anesthetics may be of some help for a fussy, crying, teething infant.

Auscultation to the heart and lungs is done in the usual manner. Palpation of the abdomen, particularly to check for the enlargement of the liver and spleen, is important at four months of age. At this ime, your doctor may pick up on organomegaly due to hemoglobinopathies, glycogen storage diseases, spherocytosis, or even neuroblastoma.

By maintaining eye contact with the infant, your doctor can estimate whether the infant can focus, follow, and see. By talking to the infant, your doctor can judge how well the infant hears. He/she stretches the infant, moves all the joints, and feels for the muscle tone. Your pediatrician may pick up some asymmetry, signifying problems in the central nervous system. The Moro reflex may be disappearing, but the tonic neck reflex may still be prominent.

Iron supplementation is a must for a four-month-old; otherwise, one can expect nutritional anemia by nine months to one year of age. Iron supplementation can be in the form of iron fortified formula or vitamin drops with iron for breastfed infants. Mixed feeding provides some iron; however, this usually is not enough for a fast growing infant. For those infants who do not tolerate iron-fortified formula, the parents may challenge the health care provider by saying that he or she forgets that their baby is "allergic" to iron. Most parents will understand the need for iron when they are told about the physiology of iron absorption and its utilization and function in the body.

The second set of immunization shots are administered at the end of the visit if the infant tolerated the first set of shots. If the parents reported any adverse reactions to the initial set of vaccines, the doctor will document it carefully in the medical record with particular reference to the nature and extent of the reaction. Some reactions are expected, and the parents may just need reassurance and be taught ways to avoid symptoms such as the high fever associated with the vaccination. Some true adverse reactions may require a modification of the vaccine schedule. Never abandon vaccination totally. One may administer diphtheria/tetanus toxoid instead of the traditional DTP if the baby reacts to the pertussis vaccine. The Food and Drug Administration has licensed the acellular pertussis vaccine for younger infants in the United States. The vaccines that your youngster will get at this visit include: Diphtheria, Tetanus, acellular Pertussis vaccines, intramuscular Poliomyelitis vaccines, conjugated Pneumococcal vaccines, and conjugated Hemophilus Influenzae Type B vaccines.

At this point, the doctor may ask the parents if they have any particular questions and concerns that have not been addressed and offer help and suggestions that may be appropriate for the family. If there are siblings around, your pediatrician will always involve them in the discussion so that they feel they are a part of the team. The doctor tells them that it is important for them to help the parents keep small toys and other objects away from the baby and not to feed or share food with the baby without adult supervision.

In closing, your pediatrician may compliment the parents and the family unit on how well the youngster is growing and developing and instruct them to make an appointment for the next visit.

The Six-Month-Old

You will find that by this time things are more routine. You are not as tired or as frustrated as you were in the earlier months of your parenthood. You will find that your baby is much more fun to be around, with much more personality. Your baby may start to express his anger, exhibited by crying or screaming, when you leave him alone. He will have a lot more interaction with you. As a matter of fact, the baby demands your attention all of the time. This is normal.

The baby is starting to develop his objective self: the self that interacts with other people. The recognition of familiar persons and the expression of anger are termed separation anxiety. It is a milestone in human development in that the development of the subjective self has been completed. As you might notice, the subjective self-development starts at birth with his eyes rolling around, then proceeding to finding his hands and feet. Ultimately, by six months of age, he is able to bring his foot to his mouth and suck his toes. The infant explores himself.

As you enter the office and register for your well check, the office personnel will greet you and direct you to the examination room. You will be instructed to undress the infant completely, including the diaper, for his measurements. These measurements, again, will be plotted on the growth curve. By six months of age, most babies have doubled their birth-weight. If there are minor deviations, do not be alarmed since it is the trend that is important rather than the absolute values. The office nurse will ask for your concerns, worries and questions, noting them down, and getting ready for your physician to come and visit with you.

When the doctor comes in, greeting you and the baby, he or she may comment on his or her first impression of the baby at this visit. The doctor may instruct you to continue holding the baby. This is because of the separation anxiety that your doctor may expect at this age of development. Then, the doctor will proceed with questioning you about how you, your baby, and your family are doing. If there are no real concerns, he or she will start asking about the feeding schedule, the tolerance of baby food, and nursing or formula feeding. The doctor may talk a little about your baby's physical growth, pointing at the growth curve and showing you how well your baby is growing.

By six months, it is all right to introduce meat. Traditionally, one introduces lean, white meats first, like turkey or chicken, before red meats. Again, there is no real scientific reason for it. One usually holds off finger foods until at least nine months of age because of the choking hazard.

Teething may be a perpetual problem at this age. An average infant cuts the first set of teeth by six to eight months of age. Of course, there will be some variations; some babies teeth earlier and some teeth later. This should not be of any concern. Late teething just means that there is less time for the deciduous teeth to rot, particularly if your baby is bottle-fed; and less tears from your eyes if you are breast-feeding, since most babies bite their mothers' nipples. Should this happen after your baby cuts the first set of teeth, you need to stop the breastfeeding and express your disapproval. After a time or two, your infant will get the message that you do not enjoy being bitten and the behavior will stop. With teeth, you may also introduce chunkier food items, the so-called second foods.

A lot of parents are amazed and alarmed to find that their babies have not gained a lot of weight compared to previous visits. There are several reasons for this. First, babies are much busier moving, stretching, rolling, and maybe even crawling. These activities use up calories, putting less into storage and weight gain. Second, babies are more easily distracted during feeding. Tiny little sounds or disturbances arouse their interest. They consume less food, particularly if they are breastfed. You will find that your infant seldom nurses more than a few minutes because of the distractions. Therefore, the calorie-rich hind milk is not secreted and utilized by the infant. Some ways to overcome this include: nurse the infant in a very quiet room, nurse during the early morning hours before everybody else wakes up, and nurse late at night after the others are asleep. With teething, your infant may have discomfort when eating. They may prefer to chew on the nipples instead. You may find that by giving small frequent feedings, your baby feels better and eats better.

Developmentally, your baby may be able to sit up briefly, leaning forward for support. He may bounce actively when you stand him upright. He grasps with much more precision and starts to transfer items from one hand to the other. He can hold, bang, and shake a rattle. The infant may rake small pellets with the whole hand, taking them to his mouth. He may start to vocalize, talking to toys and reaching for and patting mirror images. He may even vocalize "m-m-m" when he is upset and crying.

Starting at six months of age, your doctor may examine your baby while you hold the youngster in your arms or on your lap. This is because most babies will start crying when you lay them down on the examination table. However, one can still perform a comprehensive examination efficiently while the baby is sitting on the mother's lap. If you do not feel comfortable about this, please let your doctor know, so that he or she may explain the reason. The separation anxiety your baby experiences when you lay him down on the examination table may ruin the opportunity to perform a comprehensive examination. Most pediatricians learn from experience to examine a baby at this age on the lap of the parents.

Again, your doctor will start with hip abduction to check for "congenital hip dislocation" which, actually, is a misconception. The hips do not need to be congenitally malformed to be in the dislocated position. Some hips are unstable at birth. If they are not kept in the stable position in the acetabulum, the resulting joints will not develop well. Dr. Robert Salter, an orthopedic surgeon, proved this experimentally in an animal model many years ago. Thus, you will find that your doctor checks for hip dislocation at every visit during the first year of life. While your doctor is examining the hips, he or she will also check the femoral pulses, inspecting the diaper area for rashes, and feeling for the testes in boy infants while looking for the development of labial adhesion in girl infants.

After putting the diaper back on, your doctor will continue the examination in a systematic fashion. From head to toe, your doctor feels the scalp, the head and neck, behind the ears, and checks the tear ducts. Looking at your baby's eyes to see if your baby tracks, talking to your baby to see if your baby responds, and observing the movements of your baby are all part of the evaluation of the child. Then, your doctor uses the stethoscope to auscultate the heart, lungs, and the abdomen for normal and abnormal sounds, feels and palpates for the enlargement of abdominal organs, and palpates for any abnormal vibrations in the chest area, indicating pathology. Your doctor may then pull your baby into a standing position to see if your baby is ready to support weight on his or her feet. Physiologic bowed legs are normal and of no concern. As your baby grows, this will correct itself. A tincture of time is the best cure. However, pathological conditions do need attention. Sometimes, they warrant a referral to the orthopedic surgeon.

The six month check-up is the ideal time to discuss accident prevention. Your baby is a lot more mobile now. Your baby is in constant motion, grasping this and sucking that. You need a systematic method to baby-proof your house, starting with the baby's room and going through the rest of the house where the baby may be at any time of the day. Electrical outlets, electrical cords, table clothes, ornaments, decorations, houseplants, and pets are all targets of your baby's attack. Be prepared.

It is important to poison-proof your house at the same time. Drugs should be in a cabinet with locks or latches. Stoves, ovens, fire-places, heating vents, and hot water pipes should all be protected so the innocent infant does not grasp or touch them. Things under the kitchen sink should be organized and latched. A bottle of syrup of ipecac should be available in the house. Syrup of ipecac is a safe emetic. It should be used at the advice of the poison center staff or your physician. Keep the telephone number of the poison center on your telephone list or in a highly visible area so that you can locate it quickly. You can reach your local poison center by dialing 1-800-222-1222. This is a toll free number. All fifty states use this telephone number. In the case of a true emergency, call 911. Recently, the American Academy of Pediatrics advised parents not to stock syrup of ipecac at home. However, the American Association of Poison Control Centers, the American Academy of Clinical Toxicology, and the American Academy of Medical Toxicology insist that there are uses for syrup of ipecac, and it should be available in the home setting to be utilized in emergency situations.

Keep all potentially harmful products in their original containers. Labels on the original container may give first-aid instructions if someone should swallow the product. Never use drinking glasses or soft-drink bottles to store poisonous products - someone may think they are food and swallow them. Harmful products should always be stored away from food preparation areas, particularly in a farm community where pesticide and produce should be stored separately. Discard out-dated prescriptions. Store prescriptions in their original container. The prescription number will let your pharmacist identify the ingredients in the prescription. Be sure to poison-proof the grandparents' houses as well. They are sure to have more medications lying around waiting for a disaster to happen!

As indicated, separation anxiety is prominent at this age. This translates to stranger anxiety. Your cuddly baby suddenly becomes a mommy's boy and refuses to go to grandparents and friends without a big fuss and crying. This is normal. However, it takes some explaining to your friends and family, particularly grandparents, to assure them that your baby does not hate them. It is simply this stage of development that makes your baby anxious about strangers and separation. Reassure others that they are welcome to interact with the baby.

Separation anxiety also means that some babies will start waking up at night, crying for their parents. It is estimated that about fifty percent of infants do so at this stage of development. Obviously, you are disturbed. You want to cuddle the baby and console him so he will go back to sleep. You feed and rock the baby. All these are good intentions on your part, yet they are detrimental to the future development of your baby and your comfort. What you should really do is provide a night light in your baby's room so that he can see that he is in a familiar surrounding. A big picture of you and your spouse hanging in the room is helpful so the baby can see the picture and be reassured. A stereo or a radio of light music or rhythm may be soothing. Or better still, a tape recording of your voice reading or singing to your baby, playing in the baby's room may soothe the baby. You may pat the baby a few times, but resist holding, cuddling, and rocking the baby. Your baby will enjoy and demand these treatments every night. Before too long, a bad habit will form. Please do not reward a behavior that is not right, burdensome to you, and detrimental to your baby. Your goal as a parent is to let your infant grow up to be an independent person. Learning to tolerate frustration is good for your infant, no matter what time of the day it is!

You should not feed the baby at night time, either. The baby who wakes up crying should not be rewarded with a midnight snack. Instead, feed the baby before bedtime so that you are assured that your baby is not hungry. Never put a baby's bottle in his crib. You will be working to pay for the dentist's bill in the years to come. Actually, your baby is awakening because of separation anxiety rather than hunger.

Please do not be trapped into all kinds of services that you may not enjoy doing in the middle of the night. Once the baby learns that you will rock him to sleep, he will not want to go to sleep by himself. By the time you are sick and tired of the mid-night service, he will still need to break the bad habit, and you will have to put up with his protests for a number of nights. Similarly, resist the temptation of sleeping with your baby. After your baby gets used to the body warmth and cuddling, he will not want to sleep alone. It has been demonstrated that co-sleeping increases the risk of sudden infant death syndrome. Unless you want to have a communal bed with your baby for the next few years to come, do not start this bad habit.

It is not advisable to use a walker. The increased mobility increases accidents. A walker may be used with direct supervision. A playpen is very safe and is a good investment to keep your infant confined in a safe area if you need to work. When your baby sees you walking around the house and working, he will cry. It is all right to let him cry instead of holding him and working at the same time. Talk to him. Let him know that when you have free time you will play with him. Your baby will learn that you are not abandoning him. Holding your baby and trying to work at the same time is usually dangerous. Attempting to do several things at the same time may be subjecting your baby to unnecessary dangers that may injure both you and your baby.

If there are accompanying siblings at your visit, your doctor may invite them to talk about the baby. Your doctor will see if they are expressing any concerns about the baby and may tell them that they are good helpers for their parents. He or she will remind the parents that with the increased mobility of the infant, the baby will get into the turf of the older siblings and turf-wars may begin. The older siblings do not need to give in to the infant, yet the infant will eventually get even with the older ones. This approach is good for both concerned. Because the older ones need to learn to feel good about themselves, they do not need to give up their rights to the baby (or any body else.) They do not need to suppress their personal feelings and develop an inferiority complex. They do need to defend themselves and to express their feelings and opinions and be assertive.

Simultaneously, your younger one needs to learn that the world does not revolve around him. After all, he is developing the objective-self, learning to deal with other people. If he ever learns that people should always give in to him, he will become a tyrant to rule the world. Unfortunately, one day this glass bubble will burst and the mirage will fade, and your youngster will learn that there are bigger bullies around. He may have to pay dearly for what you started many years ago. Let the siblings learn to live with each other. Let them fight. At this age, you may have to take the baby to your room and tell the older ones that they hurt your feelings, thus protecting the infant. Yet please do not punish the older ones, particularly if they are still two to three years of age. They have not yet developed the concept of right or wrong, good or bad. They just know that the baby invades their turf, hurting them. Providing alternatives, separating the fighting children, and distracting them will usually calm the situation.

Your doctor may ask whether your baby had a reaction to the second set of vaccinations your baby received at the four-month visit. Any significant reaction should be reported and recorded in the medical record. Your baby will receive the third set of vaccinations at the 6 month check-up. The third set of vaccinations consists of Diphtheria, Pertussis and Tetanus, Poliomyelitis vaccines, conjugated Hemophilus Influenza B vaccine, conjugated Pneumococcal vaccine, and Hepatitis B vaccine - just like the set at two-months of age. You may also want to give your child the Influenza Vaccines starting at six months of age. It is advisable to give some antipyretics, like acetaminophen, to control the anticipated pain and temperature. This may be continued for the next twenty four to thirty six hours, at four-hour intervals.

Your doctor may then summarize the findings of the visit and invite your questions and comments. If you have a list of questions, this is a good time to go through them. Your doctor may point out the strength of your baby and compliment your parenting skills. He or she will suggest the next visit at nine months of age and ask you to set up the next appointment with the receptionist.

The Nine-Month-Old

Now that your baby is nine months old, you are entering another new era. Your baby is a lot of fun, a bundle of energy, and starts to manipulate you and your spouse. You feel like to throwing up your arms and asking, "What have I done?" Be collected, things will be all right. As you've already noticed, your baby demands your service all the time. The separation anxiety is still there. Your baby does not want to be left alone. Your baby is in constant motion. You may wonder where all this energy comes from. By the end of the day, you feel exhausted. When your baby finally falls asleep, you lie down, stretch your sore back, and tell yourself how lucky you are to have a healthy, active baby. Yet, fun continues to come your way. There are many more chapters in the life journey of your little darling.

As you step into the pediatrician's office, you are greeted with a smile and instructed to proceed to the examination area, strip the baby naked, and get ready for the nine-month check up appointment.

The office nurse will weigh and measure your baby. This time, the office nurse will probably need to use all kinds of tricks to keep the baby on the scale. Luckily, with electronic scales, measurement can be accomplished in a few seconds. Still, most infants will cry and make a big fuss about it. Measuring the length is another story. You will find the office nurse is trying to pin down a flying arrow. Please be reminded that the absolute numbers on the measurements are of no importance, the trend is what is important. Parents may wonder why their baby has not gained much weight or grown much taller. There are several reasons for this phenomenon. The inability to get exact measurements is one reason; another reason is that your baby is too busy to stay focused on eating - he is too easily distracted. More importantly, it takes a lot of calories for your baby to maintain his current activity level and the body may not be able to spare the extra calories to maintain a fast weight gain. Also, the rate of growth slows during the second half of the first year of life, so do not be alarmed by the slow weight gain by your baby.

The office nurse will ask you a few questions about your baby, recording them on the medical record, to let your doctor know.

After your baby settles down from the initial manipulations, your doctor will come in and greet you, and the whole process of the encounter begins. Your doctor may ask you questions as the usual first step while you are still holding the baby. At this point, you may anxiously want to know what is going on with your baby's weight gain and general health. In particular, you may have noticed that your baby has not been eating well for a while. What has gone wrong? What is the problem? You may find yourself feeling guilty for the poor weight gain and poor growth of your previously healthy baby. What should you do next? You doctor does not seem to be concerned at all! You may even start to doubt your doctor. Be collected. Your doctor will try to explain some of the physiological phenomena to you.

As the baby grows, the rate of growth slows down. He does not need to consume as much food as before. Now that he is aware of his surroundings, he is a lot more social and may be distracted while eating solid food, breast-feeding, or bottle feeding. The reduction in appetite and the distractions are both normal. Do not be alarmed. You need to be patient and work with your infant. Provide small, frequent feedings. Start to introduce finger foods, particularly those that may dissolve in the mouth, like teething biscuits. You need to feed the baby eight to ten times a day. By rotating different foods in the different food groups, you may still be able to feed the baby a balanced diet. For example, after the teething biscuit, you may give your baby sips of milk, either by breastfeeding or by feeding from a cup or a bottle. An hour later, you may give a piece of soft carrot, again followed by some water or juice. An hour later, give a piece of mild cheese or curds of cottage cheese followed by breastfeeding or some milk from a cup or a bottle. Finally, you may offer some deli meat or Vienna sausage.

Sausage needs to be cut into small pieces. Never give a whole sausage to an infant because he may choke and aspirate. And, the meat is very difficult to retrieve from the baby's throat. Avoid peanuts, popcorn, frozen peas, corns, raw carrot sticks, hot dogs, raw apple pieces, whole grapes, or any other item on which your infant may choke and aspirate.

There is no way to feed a nine-month-old infant all four-food groups in one sitting. You need to be innovative in feeding your baby. Feeding time should be a happy time for the baby. It should also be a pleasant experience for you. You do not need to tie your baby down and force-feed him. In that scenario, feeding becomes a punishment for both you and your baby. This may have long lasting consequences on your baby's self-development. Table manner training should not start until four or five years of age because, at this point, your baby does not have the needed attention span to sit still for a traditional meal. As you know, this requires up to thirty minutes of attention. Do not punish yourself or your baby. Mealtime should be a happy time for both of you! Your doctor may want to prescribe a vitamin with iron and fluoride supplement, particularly if you are still breastfeeding or if you are planning to switch your infant from formula to homogenized whole milk.

Now you find that your baby can sit independently indefinitely. He sits steadily, sometimes attempting to pull up on objects, like the couch, to stand. Some children can stand-alone and walk as early as this stage. They crawl well now, making themselves vulnerable to accidents, like falling and hitting their head against the coffee table. Watch out for your baby.

Your baby is curious and learning that things may fall. He may attempt to release toys, and that becomes a great game for him to play. You will find that you will pick up toys, spoons and other objects thousands of times a day. He likes to hit things, banging them. He is starting to pinch now, not meaning to hurt anybody, yet he needs to learn that it is not an acceptable behavior. You find yourself and many of your friends and relatives telling your youngster many "no-no's" in a day. This is not necessary. You can just remove him from whatever mischief and put him in a safe haven, like the play-pen. He will greet you broadly with a "mama" or "dada" when he needs you for any service, with a pitiful look asking for help. Thus, he starts to manipulate you.

Obviously, your little darling does not know right from wrong, good from bad, or danger from safety at this age. Yet, it is up to you not to let him manipulate you. You do not need to be angry and frustrated with your child. You know better. You know right from wrong, good from bad, and danger from safety. You just need to decide that you are firm in your belief and your conscience. It is perfectly all right to remove your baby from danger and put him in a safe place even if it means that your baby may cry for a period of time. Crying has never been shown to hurt a baby. Learning to tolerate frustration is good for your baby. You can console your baby; however, if you let your baby manipulate you into a dangerous situation, the regret is yours forever.

Your youngster likes to play with you and invites you to play. Pat A Cake and Peek-A-Boo are good games for this age infant. Even simply rolling on the floor and giggling with your baby is a lot of fun. When you are leaving for work or simply going to another room, your baby will wave goodbye. You will find that this gives you immense joy: the joy of a parent which no earthly treasure can replace.

Your baby becomes your inspector at this age. He can pick up the tiniest little things, no matter where they are, and put them in his mouth. You need to be meticulous. You need to always pick up the little things and run after your little one, so that he will not surprise you. His little fingers can go everywhere. Again, if your electrical outlet has not been plugged, this is the time to do so. Keys, bells, and rattles all fascinate your youngster. Play with your baby. These are the precious moments in life. If you desire, you can record all of these moments on videotape. These tapes may become your treasure as you continue to watch your baby grow for years to come.

A nine-month-old infant likes to climb up the stairs, up the couch, up your lap, and down again. This is a game for him. Be prepared, though. He likes to dive, too. Some authorities believe it is because babies do not have good depth perception. Other authorities say that it is just because they do not know any better. Thus, when you have to leave your baby for a moment, the safest place is on the floor or the playpen so that he will not fall. Again, the couch, the table, the bed, and the infant seat are all dangerous, even for a split second. All too often, it is that split second when accidents occur.

Your baby likes to play with water with all its inherent danger. He may even crawl to the bathroom and play with the water in the commode! Be sure to close the bathroom door. Teach your spouse and older children to do so, also. Another dangerous situation is five gallon containers, particularly those half-filled with water. Your baby may dive in and, with no way to get out, he may drown. Avoid these situations; empty those pails. It is neither necessary nor hygienic to keep them around.

Similarly, bathing time will be a lot of fun for your nine-month-old infant. You will enjoy splashing in the water with your baby. But, as on any slippery surface, great care should be taken. Otherwise, a joyous moment may turn into a disaster.

Be reminded not to shampoo your baby girl's hair in the bathtub. The shampoo may irritate the vaginal area, causing labial adhesion and urinary tract infections.

If you bathe your infant with older siblings, you need to supervise the bath. You cannot let the older ones be in charge because they may not appreciate the dangers that are involved.

Talk to your baby. In this way, you are teaching your baby to talk. Read and sing to him. Name objects for him so that he starts to mimic you. Always try to teach your baby to do the right thing at the right time, instead of telling him "no, no" all day long. It has been estimated that an average infant at this age receives twenty "no, no's" a day. As explained in the previous chapter, an infant cannot develop a good objective self if he is being shouted at all day long by the dearest people in his life! He will feel inadequate and be convinced that he is unable to perform any task at all. This may have a very long-lasting effect on his self-development. You need to be firm, gentle, and certain of yourself. You need to know your intent for your baby, and be consistent, so that your baby may learn. This is the stage when your baby may manipulate you to fight with your spouse. When you offend your child, he may go to your spouse and abandon you. Yet, your spouse should be supportive of you so that you both become one. Your infant will soon learn that he cannot manipulate his parents. Instead, your child will learn from you.

Some parents worry about the way their baby stands. They worry about the baby's feet. By nine months of age, as the baby pulls up to stand, he soon learns that standing up like Charlie Chaplin is not stable. Since the diaper occupies space in the groin area, your baby abducts the hip, rotates the thigh, and stands with the feet turning in. When you take off the diaper and stretch their legs (with the knee-cap pointing upwards when your baby is lying down) you will find that your baby's feet are straight. It is true that your baby could have feet deformities, but your doctor would have pointed that out to you a long, long time ago. Physiological knock-knee and physiological bowleg are both normal physiological conditions, so do not be alarmed to find that in your baby. Physiological flat-feet is also normal - one in seven children will not develop their longitudinal arch. That does not mean your baby will not walk normally. Be reassured. Shoes are used to protect the feet. Shoes should be large and non-restrictive with non-skid soles, and they should be light and comfortable. You do not need to buy expensive shoes. They will be out-grown very quickly. Barefooted people develop their feet best. When you are inside the house, it is absolutely all right to let your youngster walk barefooted.

Night terrors may still be prominent. As stated in the last chapter, this is normal. Use the technique outlined in the previous chapter to help your infant to overcome it. Do not start a bad habit.

Your doctor may then proceed to the physical examination. He or she will want to examine your baby while you are holding the child. Hip abduction, checking for the femoral pulses, observing for the diaper rashes, feeling for testicles in boys and looking for labial adhesion in girls are all done simultaneously. Then, your pediatrician may proceed to the head and neck region, feeling for abnormal findings and pointing out his or her observations to you. He or she will talk softly to your baby to see if your baby hears well, while observing the child's eye movements to see the tracking of the eyes.

Next, the doctor will auscultate the heart and lungs. It is not unusual for your doctor to find a hemic heart murmur at this stage. It only means that your baby needs more supplemental iron in his diet. It is of no consequence. The abdomen will be palpated for abnormal enlargement of organs, particularly the liver, spleen and kidneys. Sometimes, your doctor may listen for bowel sounds or other abdominal bruits for possible pathology. Your baby may resist movements, like stretching his arms and legs or massaging his back to check for curvatures. Do not be disturbed by your baby's resistance. Remember the stranger anxiety. Your baby is just not happy to be handled by a stranger.

Your doctor may then ask about the reaction to the third set of immunizations. He or she will write this in the baby's medical record. Your doctor may recommend a blood test for anemia or an electrocardiogram, particularly if he or she heard a hemic heart murmur. Your doctor may also want to do a blood lead level test, depending on your environment and your community.

If a sibling is accompanying the infant during the visit, the pediatrician will try to include the older one throughout the visit. Inviting the child to help during the examination is a good practice that shows the older children that they can help take care of the baby. Typically, the doctor will comment on how well the children behave and how much their help is appreciated.

Your doctor may discuss your next pregnancy and family planning. The best spacing is about two years between children. The regression of your older child leads children to feel like they are twins growing up together, and they will maintain this closeness for life. Discuss this with your husband. He needs to appreciate what you feel and what you think. After all, it takes both of you to cooperate to be successful in raising a family.

Finally, your doctor may ask you if you have any questions or comments on your youngster's growth. Then, he or she will suggest the next check-up to be scheduled at one year of age.

The One-Year-Old

Happy birthday! Both you and your infant have passed a milestone together. You have a lot of reasons to celebrate, many more than your youngster. Your infant does not appreciate the occasion. The child does not understand that he is supposed to perform in front of grandparents, friends, and relatives. Looking back a year ago, you were in the labor and delivery area of your hospital - hurting, sweating, screaming and anticipating. Now that your baby is healthy: playing, laughing, being passed from one guest to another, your joy is immense and is difficult to describe. Only a parent can imagine what you have been through during the first year. The pain, the suffering, and the anticipation are all well worth it. This is what perpetuates human existence. This is parenthood.

As you meander into your doctor's office for the one-year check-up, you are directed into the examination to undress your baby down to the diaper, and start the process that you are quite familiar with by this time. Looking at your baby and remembering the praises and reassurances from relatives, you feel certain that this visit will sail smoothly by without a lot of obstacles.

When the office nurse comes and takes the baby to the weight station, you are curious about the weight gain. Sure enough, your baby gains weight as expected. By one year of age, one would expect a tripling of the birth weight, about twenty-one pounds as a general rule. However, there will be some variations. Do not be too rigid on this. Some perfectly healthy babies may weigh only eighteen pounds, while some may weigh as much as thirty pounds. This individual variation is normal, particularly with breastfed infants. They normally weigh a little less than their bottle-fed counterparts.

Measuring height/length at this age is still not a precise science because your baby will hardly hold still. The trend of growth is much more important at this age than the individual numbers of the measurement.

The office nurse will obtain a brief history. If you want to ask any questions and register any concerns, you should let the nurse know so that they are recorded on the medical record. These notes will remind your doctor to discuss these issues with you during the encounter.

It may be difficult for you to confine your baby and entertain him in a new environment. The few minutes that you have to wait for your doctor can be eternally long. When your doctor comes and greets you with a friendly smile, you are relieved and happy that the waiting period is over. As your doctor comes in and greets you, he or she will visually assess the general well-being of your baby and then sit down and visit with you.

If there are any problems that really bother you, it is a good idea to let them come out early in the discussion so that you can concentrate on the later topics that your doctor may address. As you move away from early infancy, the issues that your doctor addresses may be totally different from your agenda. After a brief discussion, your pediatrician will settle down to the routine of the well-check visit.

It is common to discuss the growth curve first as in previous visits. Your doctor will point out on the percentile charts how your baby compares to the national average, pointing out the trend of growth. It is normal to find that there is a phenomenon termed "regression towards the mean," meaning that your baby may move from the higher percentile to the median, or from the lower percentile to the mean. This is because 67% of the population will occupy the region between the 25th percentile and the 75th percentile. Again, the percentile chart is a measure of how your baby compares with other normal babies of the same age and sex.

It is not 25% of normal or 75% of normal, etc. As pointed out before, unfortunately, the common percentile charts do not take into consideration race, geographic location, culture, and feeding practices. The current percentile charts that are in use were compiled during the late fifties and early sixties. Today, the practice of infant feeding is different, and the adoration of obese infants has changed. If you are concerned about your baby's weight gain and growth, discuss it with your doctor rather than just worrying about it.

You may have already noticed that feeding is a big question, both for you and all the relatives that came to your birthday party. Developmentally, a one-year-old infant has an attention span of about 1 to 1½ minutes. There is no good way that a parent can stuff all four food groups down any infant at one time. The advice is to feed your baby often with small snacks rather than big meals.

As discussed in the previous chapter, by rotating the four food groups in succession, you can manage to provide an adequate diet for your baby. After each snack, when appropriate, you can give either homogenized whole milk, juice, or water. An average infant may consume as little as sixteen ounces of milk a day. However, some infants, particularly if still bottle-fed, may take as much as thirty-six to forty ounces. You will also find that those who drink a lot of milk will invariably consume less food. You only need to restrict milk consumption and wean off the bottle to find your baby will suddenly develop a much better appetite. Milk drinking is no longer essential after the first year of life. Restrict milk intake to less than four to six ounces a day and you will find that your baby's appetite improves readily and he eats much better.

Offer food on a constant basis, and you will find that your baby grows normally. Offer snacks to your baby continuously, practically every hour. You will find that your baby is a lot happier eating and playing with you. Finger feeding is perfectly fine. Your baby typically resists the confinement of the high chair. He will fight for your spoon. It is not necessary to perform all your previous feeding duties anymore. Let your baby enjoy eating.

Avoid food that may be hazardous for your infant. This includes nuts, particularly peanuts, popcorn, peas, beans, raw carrots, raw apples, raisins, whole grapes, and whole hot-dog sausages. Your infant may choke on any one of these items, and they are difficult to retrieve when aspirated. Vitamin supplementation, iron supplementation, and when appropriate, fluoride supplementation are essential at this stage of development.

You may want to wean your baby from breastfeeding. You can wean the baby to a cup instead of a bottle. Those that are on a bottle should also consider weaning from the bottle to a cup. The later the baby is weaned, the harder to wean the baby, both from the breast and from the bottle. A sipping cup or drinking from a straw is better for the infant. Yes, your infant may be messy, but you will need to cross this bridge sooner or later. If you do it now, you may save yourself a big dental bill in the years to come.

Developmentally, a twelve-month-old infant may be walking unaided. However, a majority of the infants can only do so by cruising along furniture, walking with one hand held, and sometimes, standing momentarily alone. All these are normal. It actually depends on how much the infant was held during the earlier months of his life. If youngsters are allowed to cruise around early, they will start walking early unless there are some pathological reasons to hinder the development. Moreover, if the youngster is held all the time with no opportunity to stand or even touch the floor, obviously, he will not be able to walk early.

Walking does not cause physiological bowlegs, rather it is a physiological feature and of no concern. Early walking increases mobility and encourages accidents since the youngster really does not know what might be dangerous. Look out for the infant. As the youngster starts to walk, you will notice that he does not walk like you or any other adult. An infant's feet point out initially, prompting a Charlie Chaplin-like walk. Obviously, this gait is not stable, and soon you may find that one foot turns in, followed by the other, so that the infant walks "pigeon-toed."

This causes concern for a lot of parents. Are my baby's feet normal? Be reassured. Because the baby wears a thick diaper that occupies a lot of space in the groin area, the hips are abducted. With the hips abducted, the feet automatically point outward. Yet, this is an unstable position. Soon, your baby learns to adduct the hip to accommodate the diaper, thus turning the feet inward, walking "pigeon-toed." If you want to be reassured, all you need to do is to remove the diaper. Align the knee-cap to face the ceiling. You will find that the feet are straight, pointing to the ceiling, too. There are situations like congenital club feet and metatarsal adductus deformity. However, if your doctor has been checking for these conditions, he or she will have noticed them long ago and appropriate therapy will have been instituted, normally during the early newborn period.

As your baby starts to walk, particularly outside the home environment, you need to protect the feet with some kind of covering. Shoes need to be soft, non-skid, porous and flexible, and large enough not to restrict the growth of the feet. They do not need to be expensive. Sandals, moccasins, soft tennis shoes, and flexible exercise shoes are all adequate. Those hard top, high top walking shoes are not necessary. They are uncomfortable and are usually too restrictive for the infant's foot development.

Your infant can pick up small objects with precision as the hands are now coordinated enough to place one block on top of the other. This is also the time when infants like to see things fall, be it from the table to the floor or from a hand to a cup. This usually becomes a favorite game for the one-year-old infant. He likes to play with you, giving objects to you at your request, and transporting objects to another person. He will offer objects to others, sometimes even to the mirror image. It is a lot of fun to play with the youngster at this age. Sometimes, he may cooperate with you when you give him specific instructions, like changing diapers or putting on clothes. His cognitive development is clearly appreciable at this age.

The physical examination will proceed in the normal fashion. With the baby totally undressed, the doctor will observe the baby's behavior, activity, and interaction with his caretaker. While the diaper is down, the doctor will check for diaper rash, hip abduction, testicles in boys, and labial adhesion in girls as explained in the previous chapter. Your doctor will feel for the enlargement of lymph glands and rough skin areas for eczema. He or she will continue to talk to the infant and observe the hearing acuity and visual response of the baby. It is difficult to do a complete vision and hearing examination, yet one can judge from one's observation on the senses of the infant.

Next, your doctor will auscultate the heart and lungs, feel the abdominal contents, look at the tympanic membranes, and check the oral cavity for teething problems, thrush, and the motility of the tongue. He/she will also observe the phonation of the infant, and from history obtained from the parents, estimate the vocabulary of the infant. A one-year-old infant can say about two words with meaning plus "mama" for mother and "dada" for father. Letting the infant walk along any furniture in the examination room tests muscle strength and joint motility.

As the youngster becomes more mobile, both inside and outside the house, one needs to watch the baby constantly. Infants are ever trusting, with no fear or appreciation of danger. Your child is totally dependent on the caretaker's common sense. The concept of baby proofing the house should be performed well before the youngster reaches one year of age. Be reassured. You cannot baby-proof the world! Be watchful, particularly when you and your baby are in the yard, outside the house area.

However, you just cannot baby-proof the whole world. Instead, you need to keep a constant eye on the infant, no matter where he is. If you are unable to do so, the safest place for the infant is in the confinement of a playpen. When you need to do something and are unable to keep an eye on the baby, then it is absolutely all right to put the baby in the playpen for a few minutes, finishing whatever you need to do before you entertain your baby again. This is not cruel. On the other hand, if you let your baby venture into an area not directly under your observation, he may be injured in the blink of an eye. Answering the telephone or the door bell, or just simply going to turn off the stove may give the baby enough time to harm himself. Please eliminate the chance for your baby to get hurt by putting him in the playpen for a few minutes. It is not cruel to the baby. A one-year-old baby can be very demanding. He can be very possessive and may not want you to leave. Letting the baby cry for a few minutes is better than letting him get hurt.

Your infant car seat may become too small for your infant. By about twenty pounds of body weight, most car seat manufacturers recommend turning the infant car seat to face the front. It is important to position the car-seat in a passenger seat in the back of a sedan because the new air bags in the front seat may suffocate the infant when inflated - or the force of inflation of the air-bag may injure the infant. Read and follow the manufacturer's instruction. It is important for you to do so.

Play with your baby creatively. Dream up games both of you will enjoy. Rolling around on the floor, letting the baby ride on you, or rolling your baby around on top of a big beach ball are good exercises for you and your baby. Reading is a good game. Be mindful that your baby's attention span is very short and be prepared to change from one action to another every few minutes. Otherwise, you may become frustrated that your baby does not enjoy playing as much as you do.

You need to set some goals and provide limits for your baby since he does not know the rules, right from wrong, or good from bad. It is up to you to teach these concepts. Be persistent. Instead of screaming "no, no" all day, be assertive and persistent by removing him from any situation you do not think is right or safe. He will eventually learn. You do not need to get upset, either. After all, he is just beginning to learn. Be patient with your baby as he has no intent to upset you, at least not at this age.

Your infant will soon become a toddler. It will be fun and challenging. Just be prepared, anticipate the change, foresee the danger, and you will have many enjoyable years to come. If you have any questions, do not hesitate to ask your doctor-he or she is there to serve you.

In closing, your doctor may then ask if you have any other questions or problems. If there are no more questions, your baby will be given a Tuberculosis intra-dermal skin test along with the chicken pox vaccine. Tuberculosis has been on the rise in the past few years. It is advisable to screen for it at one year of age, particularly before the baby gets the measles, mumps and rubella vaccines. Even though chicken pox is a fairly benign illness, it is advisable to have the vaccine since each year there are approximately three hundred deaths attributed to the complications of chicken pox. Both the Academy of Pediatrics and the American Public Health Association agree that the chicken pox vaccine should be given to infants at one year of age if they have not already had chicken pox, and they do not have any contraindications to life attenuated vaccines. Other vaccines may be given at the same time, like the Measles, Mumps and Rubella Vaccine, the booster DTaP vaccines, the conjugated Pneumococcal vaccines, Hemophilus Influenza B vaccines, and the Poliomyelitis Vaccines. It should be noted that about 20% of the time, after the MMR vaccine, your infant will develop a temperature for two to three days from the sixth to the tenth day after vaccination. A fine, macular rash may follow. This should not be of concern. It is a reaction from the live, attenuated Measles vaccine. You may control the fever with the appropriate dosages of acetaminophen or ibuprofen, and put calamine lotion on the rash, if necessary.

The next appointment will be at fifteen months of age. The parent is advised to set up the appointment before leaving the office.

The Fifteen-Month-Old

Another three months have passed and you find yourself with your baby back in the doctor's office for the fifteen month checkup. This time you are probably armed with a series of questions because your little darling is now a toddler, getting into anything and everything. You may need some suggestions and guidance to work with your baby. Your doctor is there to help you, offering suggestions and guidance so that you may obtain some insight into the next few months of your toddler's life.

Before you even step into the office, you may find that your baby throws a fit as you turn the corner, entering the familiar sight of the office. Your baby remembers! This is the doctor's office. This is a strange place as far as the baby is concerned. A typical fifteen-month-old baby has a significant memory. You cannot fool him as easily as before.

The receptionist greets you with a smile, anticipating that you will have a fight with your youngster when she asks you to take the baby to the examination room to undress. At that age, it is still customary to weigh and measure the infant naked. It is the naked weight and length that are recorded and plotted on the growth curve, making a fair comparison. Your baby will protest and the office nurse may need to peel him out of your lap to perform the measurement. Your baby may scream, kick, and throw a big temper tantrum.

This is normal and to be expected. Your baby is now much stronger and also experiencing the second stage of separation anxiety. Be reassured that the office nurse will not deliberately hurt your baby. She is a professional, trained to do her job. Trust her. She may be talking to your baby, holding him, encouraging you to distract the baby. Sometimes she may even ask you to step into the examination (exam) room so that the baby does not see you for a few minutes and will settle down so she can complete this task. Another common method is to ask you to hold the baby and weigh and then weigh you alone subtracting your weight from the combined weight to give the weight of the toddler. This, however, is not the preferred method because the scale for adults is not as precise as the infant scale and one may not be able to record down to ounces using the adult scale. At least, this may give us a measure of the trend of how your baby is gaining weight.

Similarly, for the length and head circumference measurements, the office nurse may need to recruit your help in holding your youngster. From all this, you may be able to appreciate that measuring a toddler is an art rather than a precise science. It is good to remember that it is the trend of growth that is important; the individual number carries much less weight in the interpretation of the growth curve.

As your doctor comes in and greets you while you are trying to settle your baby, your baby may flare up and cry again. This is normal and you do not need to apologize. Your doctor should understand. Holding your baby on your lap can still permit a meaningful interview and examination. You can express concerns and questions that have been bothering you as your baby is settling down. Discussing the questions that you want answered will provide an opportunity for you to set the tone for the visit. Common questions include the behavior of your youngster, particularly around strangers, eating habits, defiance and oppositional behavior, and the curiosity of the toddler.

It is advisable for you to prepare a list of questions so that all areas are covered. Your doctor may or may not be able to cover all the concerns; he or she may refer you to other specialists in child development or may want you to schedule a conference outside the office visit because these topics each may deserve an hour's discussion, and your doctor may not be able to fit them all into the office visit. Do not feel offended if your doctor makes this suggestion. He or she is just trying to be honest with you. Your doctor may also have an agenda for this particular visit.

It is common for your doctor to discuss the feeding schedule. This topic is on most parents' list at this age. You wonder why your toddler simply does not eat. He plays, cruises, walks, talks, and appears happy and well nourished, but he just will not sit down and eat like you want him to do. Be reassured. This is totally normal.

Actually, you do not need to force your child to eat. When toddlers are hungry and there is food around, they will eat enough to survive and grow. A normal, hungry baby will eat anything. If you watch the news clippings of famines in different parts of the world, you will realize that children are survivors. They do not have any preconceived ideas about what tastes good or bad. They will simply eat anything when they are hungry. All you need to do is provide the food when they are hungry. Since they still have a very short attention span, finger feeding is the best method. As described in the last few chapters, you need to provide different food groups at each feeding. You just cannot force all four food groups down in any one setting. Mealtime should be a happy time for you and your toddler. You do not need to tie him down on the high chair to have a meal! Bottle-fed toddlers should be weaned to a cup. A toddler should not be allowed to carry a bottle around all the time. Your toddler will not eat if the bottle of milk provides the entire fluid intake and nutritional requirements. Moreover, toddlers may develop significant dental problems if they depend on the bottle during the second year of life. Furthermore, it is much harder to wean them when they get older. If, at the age of fifteen months, your child still receives the bottle, by three or four years of age, your child will be able to fix his own bottle and lay down to enjoy it. You will find that to be an expensive habit when you bring your child to see his dentist.

Some mothers may still want to breastfeed their baby. It is all right to nurse your baby for comfort. Yet, you need to be reminded that if you do not insist, your baby will want to nurse whether it is convenient for you or not. A four-year-old boy may tear apart his mother's blouse, wanting to be breastfed in public. If you do not want to be embarrassed or intimidated by your child, you may want to wean before he grows too strong for you to handle.

Soft table foods are perfect for the toddler. You do not need to pre-pare separate meals for your toddler. At the same time, you do not need to spend money on expensive baby food any more. The so-called "third food" is totally unnecessary for your toddler. Foods should not be too salty, spicy, hot or gluey, or they will be difficult for the baby. Simple table foods that all members of the family consume will suffice. Avoid nuts, peanuts, hard carrot sticks, hard apple pieces, hot-dogs, corn, peas, popcorn, and hard candy. All are dangerous for a toddler. They may be easily aspirated, requiring a trip to the hospital for bronchoscopy to retrieve them from the trachea or bronchi!

Most fifteen-month-old babies can walk independently, but they still may not be too steady. They try to climb up and down the couch or steps, and some even attempt to run. They are fully mobile! Their little fingers go everywhere, picking up little things on the floor. They pick up toys with precision, casting them or putting them into a can or bottle. They stack up blocks, one or two at a time, making a tower of two. They put cubes in and out of a cup independently. They play with crayons and markers, imitating strokes and drawing pictures.

They are vocal, and you can expect them to say at least four to six words that you understand. They can say and wave bye-bye. They can even say "thank you" at times. They like to point to the things they want and demand service. They like to cast objects and throw them for you to pick up. They may even be able to indicate a wet diaper to the care-takers. They are a bundle of fun to watch and play with. Parents may want to record these precious mo-ments with video recorders to preserve the happy times to be reviewed in the years to come.

Your doctor will perform a comprehensive physical examination. Typically, this is done while you are holding the baby on your lap since no one wants to stir up separation anxiety and ruin the opportunity for a good examination. Hip abduction is no longer important since one can observe the toddler walk. However, checking the diaper area for diaper rashes, the femoral pulses, and the testis in boys and labial adhesions in girls is still essential. Your doctor may also want to check the groin areas for hernias since the inguinal region is a common place to have an indirect inguinal hernia. Next, starting from scalp and hair down, the doctor inspects, feels, palpates, and auscultates the different organs and systems. Always last will be the examination of the ear, throat, and oral cavity. This is because invariably the youngster will put up a fight.

Your doctor may need to teach you how to clean the external canal of the ears. Do not use a Q-tip - this pushes the ear wax further into the canal Rather, by using an over-the-counter wax softener and a bulb syringe, you can flush the wax from the toddler's ear without much problem. During an examination, your doctor may need to use an instrument to scoop out the wax in order to look at the ear drum. This is a common procedure. You do not need to be afraid and anxious. Your doctor will instruct you on what to do to facilitate this procedure. Your baby will not like this, but he will survive it. After all, the purpose of the entire check-up is to find out how he is doing. You need to help your doctor.

Safety is an important issue at this age, be it at home, in the yard outside, or at the playground. Your toddler needs to be watched constantly. He does not know any better. He does not have any fear and really does not know what fear means. It is you, the adult companion, that knows what danger is and how it will affect your loved ones. You need to be aware that any instance can adversely affect your baby. Simple falls happen daily. Putting things in the mouth is a constant battle. You find yourself constantly fighting with your toddler. You may want to scream at your youngster. Typically, this is the stage where you may yell twenty "no-nos" to your baby in one day. This is not necessary, and is often of no use, since he does not know the meaning of "no." To him, it is just another word that you use often. Physically removing him from danger is a much better strategy.

Yes, toddlers will throw temper tantrums. It is absolutely all right to let your child throw a temper tantrum. This will not hurt your toddler. It only teaches him that you will not tolerate his manipulation. This will also provide an opportunity for him to learn to accept and tolerate his frustration.

Tolerance of one's frustration is an important milestone in our development. As you can see, all of us have frustrating moments. We cannot throw up our arms and walk away; we need to learn to handle the situation. Similarly, your youngster needs to learn that throwing a temper tantrum will not solve anything - only that mother or father or other care-takers will just walk away, leaving them to learn to tolerate their own frustration. Learning to tolerate one's frustration is an essential step in one's psychological development. You should help to facilitate it, rather than caving in to all the demands of your toddler. After all, it is impossible to fulfill a toddler's demand all of the time.

When possible, one should continue baby-proofing and poison-proofing the house. This is particularly important now that your toddler can visit any place without you even noticing. Close all the rooms that you do not want your youngster to wander in, particularly the bathroom where your child may be attracted to water. At the same time, baby-proof and poison-proof all the houses that your youngster may visit, including the houses of grandparents, friends, relatives, and even baby-sitters. This is important, particularly the grandparent's house. They may have medications lying around that is handy for them and forget to put it up before their grandchild comes to visit. The general rules apply to their house as much as to your own house.

It is also important to remember that your toddler will have no respect for holidays or celebrations. These times are just more chances for trouble. There needs to be a new round of baby proofing during winter, Christmas, Thanksgiving, Halloween etc. Use your common sense. It is practically impossible to name all the dangerous situations. Some good advice is to be on the alert at all times because at the blink of an eye something unexpected may happen. To be on the safe side, be a little bit more restrictive and you will have a safe toddler.

Vaccinations are given for the fifteen-month-old if they were not given at one year of age. These include measles, mumps and rubella; diphtheria, tetanus, and pertussis booster; poliomyelitis booster; and conjugated hemophilus influenza B booster vaccines. Ninety-five percent of toddlers develop immunity to the measles vaccine if it is given at this age compared to only sixty-seven percent at one year of age. The American Academy of Pediatrics suggests giving this vaccine at this age in non-endemic areas for this reason.

If you have any further questions, ask your doctor before concluding this visit. And finally, your doctor may wish you good luck and hope that you survive this stage of childhood development. He or she may suggest that you not forget to make the eighteen-month appointment.

The Eighteen-Month-Old

An oppositional eighteen-month-old can fight you at any moment. Going to the doctor's office is no exception. You may find that your eighteen-month-old toddler really puts up a fight about going to the doctor's office. This may be a big concern to you. You may ask yourself why go to the doctor's office, after all, your baby is not sick. This is a common question and deserves an answer.

During the past three months or so, your youngster has changed quite a bit. He has his own personality. He expresses his feelings freely. When you turn around, you find your baby either tries to get into trouble or is throwing a temper tantrum. You are in a constant state of anxiety until you put him to sleep at night.

Some mothers who stay home with their toddlers complain to their spouses that their jobs are a double shift all the time, starting at six or seven o'clock in the morning and ending at nine or ten o'clock at night! Some working mothers feel that their true work starts when they get off work and are at home with their toddler. Their office work is break time for them! Living with a toddler is tough. He will not reason with you. He is in constant motion. He needs constant supervision; otherwise he may be in trouble in the blink of the eye. He is strong and difficult to deal with. He likes to throw temper tantrums for no apparent reason! At times, you feel only despair. You need someone to cheer you up and let you know that it is all worth it while you learn how to work with a toddler at this age. Your doctor is there to guide you, giving you new insight into the psychological development of your toddler. He or she will show you ways to tame your toddler without losing your sanity.

When you show up at the doctor's office, the receptionist, instructing you to undress the toddler, directs you to the examination room. He may not want to be undressed. This is a normal behavior. He does not know why he needs to be undressed to weigh. He will not hold still for a minute. The office nurse has to use all kinds of tricks to simply weigh and measure him. As you can imagine, the weight and length are more of an estimate than an exact measurement. However, this is acceptable because it is the trend of growth that should be emphasized rather than the exact value as indicated in the previous chapters. You want to know how he well he is growing since you have been concerned about the way that he eats.

As your doctor enters the room, you find that he or she knows how you feel and what you think. After a brief greeting, he or she will inquire how things have been going for the past three months. You may, at this point, pour out your questions and concerns going through them one at a time. Your doctor should be able to reassure you and explain some of the physiological and psychological phenomena your baby is going through.

Your doctor may then proceed to obtain a nutritional history of your child pointing out that your baby is growing normally. If you have been following his or her advice on feeding, you should be at ease knowing that meal time has been fun for you and your baby. Surely, you are glad to see that your baby falls in the normal range of the growth curve. Some parents are still worried about the eating habits of their child. As indicated, an eighteen-month-old has an attention span of about two minutes whether he is eating, playing, listening to your story, reading a book, or watching television.

Eating is no different. You find that your toddler snacks all day long. This is all right provided that you choose healthy snacks rather than just providing a bag of cereal for your toddler to snack on for the whole day. You need to rotate the four food groups as outlined in the previous chapter so that your toddler will have a balanced diet and not develop nutritional deficiencies. Always supplement the diet with a multiple vitamin plus iron to ensure appropriate nutrition.

Your toddler should definitely be on a cup by now. It is undesirable to have your toddler still on a bottle. This is because your child may carry it anywhere, laying down to suck the bottle, and create a whole hosts of problems like positional otitis or rotten milk-bottle teeth. Furthermore, it invites contamination and intestinal infections.

Table foods are fine to feed your toddler. You do not need to cook separate meals for your toddler. Offer small portions rather than throwing food away, you can always add a few more bites. As indicated above, snacking is acceptable for a toddler. After all, table manners cannot and should not be enforced until he or she is about five years old! Mealtime should be fun for you and your toddler. Your toddler needs to learn to enjoy meal times.

Next, your doctor may discuss development of the baby. By now, your baby should walk well and attempt to run. He can climb upon a chair and then to the table with no fear. He can sit in a chair steadily. He likes to play with balls and dolls. He can hurl a ball in standing position. He can stack three or four blocks on top of each other making a tower. He talks with meaning. Though he jabbers, he may have a vocabulary of more than ten words. He likes to read books, pointing at pictures selectively, and turning the pages two to three at a time. He likes to play with crayons, imitating strokes and circles. He may obey orders and carry out simple instructions. He likes to carry and hug dolls and pull toys on a string. A transitional object is a good thing for him to have. This serves as his security. He can feed himself with some spilling. He is messy! He wants to do things for himself. He is defiant, wanting to be independent. He will pull you to different places to get things for him, demanding services. He may imitate your voice, pointing at things and jabbering.

You need to be patient and work with him. Talk to him instead of just doing what he wants you to do. Give him the words and he will imitate and learn. Try to have him follow you and talk so that you can introduce new words to him. At times, he needs you to repeat the same thing many times before he can do it, just like any person learning a new technique. Have him try to do things for himself. This builds his confidence. An eighteen-month-old toddler is still forming his objective self: the "self" that determines how he will interact with people and how he will think and feel about himself. You want him to feel positive about himself. Teach him. Let him know that you are there for him. Guide him to do the right thing at the right time so that he feels good about himself. Most of all, an eighteen-month-old toddler is fun to play with!

As usual, the physical examination proceeds systematically. Hip abduction is no longer essential Instead, your doctor will observe your toddler walking. "Toeing-in" is rather common, but your doctor will check for tibia torsion and femoral torsion. Your doctor will still check for undescended testis in boys and labial adhesion in girls. And, he or she will look for diaper rash and check the hernial orifices for abnormal swellings in the inguinal area. From the scalp down, your doctor will check for eczema - on the eyebrows, behind the ears, and underneath the chin are common areas to find eczematous eruptions. A simple hydrocortisone cream will take care of most of it. However, resistant eczema may require a visit to the dermatologist for further management. The doctor feels for lymph gland enlargements around the cervical chain and palpates the mastoid area for tenderness.

Your doctor will place his hands on the toddler's abdomen to feel for enlargement of the abdominal organs, particularly the liver and spleen. He or she will palpate the kidneys. It is rather difficult to feel the kidneys unless there are pathological conditions like hydronephrosis or tumors of the kidney. However, if one does not make a routine search for these pathologies, one may not be able to recognize when what he or she is feeling is abnormal. Your doctor will auscultate the chest for normal heart sounds and listen for any murmur or arrhythmia that may develop any time during the toddler years. He or she will listen for breath sounds and air exchange if the patient is not screaming at the time. Finally, he/she will look at the tympanic membranes for their color and mobility and at the mouth for the development of the teeth and tonsils. As you try to soothe the toddler, your doctor may discuss several important issues with you which are particularly pertinent to this age. Obviously, safety is an essential topic. Your toddler knows no danger. He may dash out of the house if you leave the door open and may run to greet your running vehicle. Knowing that his parents are coming home, he gets excited and runs towards you, not knowing that you may not be able to see him as your car approaches. Always drive slowly, particularly when you are getting close to the driveway of your home. Watch out for your toddler!

Do not leave a toddler unattended at any time. In particular, when you are getting ready to bathe him in the bathroom, you need to be careful that your toddler does not dive in before you are ready. Hot water heaters should be turned down to the low setting or no more than one hundred twenty degrees Fahrenheit (120° F). At this temperature, it will take about ten minutes before your baby sustains a significant burn. At the higher settings, above hundred fifty degrees Fahrenheit (150° F), it only takes ten seconds to get a third degree scald.

You are advised to "poison-proof" your house. The effort you put in when your baby was six-months-old needs to be updated. Your toddler may be able to get into many more things now than when he was only six-months-old. You need to move any items that your toddler may ingest out of his reach. Cabinets under the kitchen sink and drawers for pots and pans need to be latched. Keep a bottle of Syrup of Ipecac in the drug cabinet in case your youngster accidentally ingests any poisonous substance. Always consult the poison center at 1-800-222-1222 or your doctor before you use the syrup of ipecac. There are indications and contraindications for the use of syrup of ipecac at home. Always be prepared.

Family pets are fun for your toddler. However, they may also be dangerous to an ever-trusting toddler. When your family dog is asleep, the dog may not know that your toddler just wants to pet him! Your lovely pet may feel that he is under attack and try to defend himself! Separate your toddler from pets when you cannot supervise them. This will prevent heartbreaks, trips to the emergency room, and other unnecessary expenses. Family pets may carry diseases and parasites too, even indoor dogs and cats will not be immune to mice or rats that come in via the garage. Fully immunize your pets.

Your toddler now shows his temper regularly. Ignore temper tantrums. Do not feed into his temper tantrum; this will let him cool down. Simply placing him in a safe place and walking away is an effective way to deal with a temper tantrum. If you are in the shopping mall when he decides to throw a tantrum, carry him to the car and let him settle down. The next time you go shopping consider leaving your toddler with a baby-sitter to avoid a similar situation. Your toddler will eventually learn. He may bang his head, hold his breath sometimes even turn blue and pass out, or bite himself. If he decides to bite you, you need to let him know that he hurt you and has to kiss you so you will feel better. By replacing the action that you do not want with an action that you prefer, you teach your toddler what is acceptable and what you will not tolerate. Be explicit and let your toddler know what he did wrong followed by some reinforcement actions, so that he knows that is exactly what mother or father means. You need to be firm. However, you do not need to be angry since he still does not know right from wrong at this stage of his cognitive development.

Spanking him only teaches him to be violent. He will think that when mother or father is angry he will be spanked, rather than that he is wrong and deserves a spanking. Worst of all, this demonstrates to him that when he is angry, he can hit people, copying what you have done to him. He will learn to model your behavior!

Most toddlers develop separation anxiety again at this age. He will not go to strangers without a fuss. "Strangers" may include grandparents, close friends, and relatives. You may need to explain to them ahead of time that this is what your toddler is experiencing to avoid uneasy feelings. A toddler who sleeps fretfully at night probably does so because of separation anxiety. When he wakes in the middle of the night, try not to let him come to your bed and sleep. Go to his room to comfort him. A night light and some music may help. On average, one out of two toddlers climb out of their crib at this age. It is advisable to keep them on the daybed or on a mattress on the floor rather than risking a fall. Resist the temptation to sleep with your child. Once he gets used to body warmth and cuddling, he may refuse to sleep alone. It is not necessary to rock him to sleep for the same reason. By providing reassurance and petting, most of the time this stage will pass easily. However, it normally takes about three weeks. Do not give in to his demands. Consistency is the key. Both parents need to agree upon the way of management before the youngster gets to this stage. Otherwise, your toddler may find your Achilles' heel in this regard! A transitional object may be helpful. You should encourage him to find a blanket, a doll, or a truck as the transitional object. This can save you a lot of trouble in the middle of the night.

Some toddlers are ready to be toilet-trained. When he indicates to you that he needs to use the bathroom, by all means bring him there and let him perform for you. However, do not force him to do so. If you ever alienate him, he will show you that using the bathroom is totally under his control and you cannot order him around. When it becomes a power struggle, you will lose! You can, however, invite him to go to the bathroom with you while you demonstrate to him. If he follows your example, all is fine. If not, it is all right too. With this attitude, you will find that your toddler can be toilet trained without any tears. Be reminded that about fifty percent of three-year-old toddlers are not completely toilet-trained, particularly at night. You do not need to be in a hurry.

If you have any further questions, ask your doctor to clarify the issues. You may want to make a special appointment to discuss parenting issues in detail with your doctor.

In closing, your doctor may comment on how well your youngster is growing and developing. Your doctor should remind you to look at the big picture as your youngster grows and suggest the next appointment at two years of age.

The Two-Year-Old

Your child may enjoy his second birthday party much more than the first one. He is normally more excited than at last year's party, much more active, and play an active roll in the party. Your relatives and friends, particularly the grandparents, are all amazed by the performance of your child. You are very proud of him. A videotape recording of this event is essential for you to recall the good times you had with your toddler. A videotape will also serve as a documentary of his development and achievement at this age.

Your toddler has a fairly complex set of personality traits by now. During the party, you probably recorded laughter, crying episodes, funny behaviors, and, most of all, temper tantrums. These so-called "terrible two" behaviors are typical for this stage of development. Your two-year-old still does not know exactly why things are done, how things are done, and what things are. Cognitively speaking, he still lacks the concept of right and wrong, good and bad, and sequencing and consequences.

Your child is trying to be very independent and wants to experience everything whether you allow it or not. You may find that most of the time you are very negative and so is your toddler. You may be hearing "no, no" from your child as much as you have been saying "no, no". He is much more difficult to distract and will go right back to what you do not want him to do. This is perfectly normal. Be reassured. Accept your child. Soon, he will learn the appropriate behavior from your modeling. Most of us learn from our parents at this stage of development.

Two-year-old toddlers are at a fun age. They do not have any worries at all. Every episode is a new experience for them. They are curious, wanting to participate in everything you are doing whether you want them to or not. However, it is advisable to involve your toddler in positive activities so that you can have more interaction with him and teach him.

As you are walking into the doctor's office with your two-year-old, depending on his past experience with your pediatrician's office, you may find that your toddler is unwilling to go in. You may have to drag him into the office. However, if the relationship between your toddler and the staff of the office is a positive one, you may find that your toddler obediently follows you to the office without much of a fight. The receptionist will direct you to the examination room where you will undress your toddler, getting ready for the nursing staff to weigh and measure your youngster.

It is important to have accurate weight and height measurements this time. Most two-year-old youngsters can stand on the scale to be weighed and measured. Standing height is important. By doubling this height, one can roughly predict the ultimate height of the individual. To a certain degree, this prediction is true. By two years of age, most toddlers weigh about 28 pounds. Most boys are taller than girls. On average, boys are around 35 to 36 inches and girls are around 32 to 33 inches. The office nurse may ask you for your questions and prepare for the doctor to come in for the interview and the examination.

When the doctor comes in and greets you and your toddler, the doctor may pay more attention at first to your toddler to see how your child reacts to him/her. If the toddler's response is negative, the doctor may want you to hold the youngster so that you can comfort your child while the doctor talks to you. If your youngster's reaction is positive, the doctor may want to chat a little with the toddler to gain his or her confidence before the examination. An interval history is then obtained.

You may want to voice any concerns and problems you have encountered with your little darling for the past six months. Now that your child is an individual with his own character and personality, you find that your child is very strong-willed and determined to do whatever he sets out to do. You may also find that your emotions are in constant turmoil. You may not know how to deal with your child. Be confident. You have come to the right place for guidance. Your pediatrician will help you find answers and shed light on your perplexing problems with your little darling.

Your feelings are normal. Two-year-old children have no respect for anybody; they are only interested in their own world. You do not need to feel intimidated by your toddler. Be firm and gentle. You do not need to give in to his demands. Yet, always be ready to guide your child to do the right things at the right time. Time-out may be an effective tool if you use it correctly. The key is that you need to be in control; otherwise, your toddler will see that you are going to lose your temper instead.

One method that has been shown to be effective is to tell your youngster that, for whatever reason, he has annoyed you, and you are going to go to your room, close the door to rest, and try to feel better. Typically, your youngster will throw a temper tantrum outside your door. You need to wait until all the crying stops, then open the door and go out. You will find that your little darling will be ready to reconcile with you and hug you so you will feel better!

This method is much better than ordering your youngster to go to the corner, the "naughty chair", or the bedroom. When you do this, your child will invariably come right at you, making you angrier, and you will lose control. Moreover, you do not want your youngster to feel that his room is his personal jail! His own room should be a place of comfort rather than a place of punishment! Otherwise, one day your child will refuse to go into his room, stating that he is a good boy and does not need to go to his room for a time-out! Like Dr. Edward Christopherson says, you need to have "timing-in," to contrast with "timing-out," meaning that you need to provide moments when your youngster looks forward to your presence and having fun, to contrast with the moments you are not available. Typically, a two-year-old only needs a two-minute time-out period. The general rule is one minute per year of age for a time-out.

You can also use "I" messages to let your youngster know how you feel when he misbehaves. The "I" message consists of four components: it starts with "when you do such and such," I feel "describe your feeling," "because of a reason," followed by "I would like you do this thing instead of the action that offended me." This message gives a direct statement to your youngster about how you feel, what went wrong, and how to correct it. It is very powerful because you are teaching your toddler how he can offend and upset you. At the same time, you are teaching your child how to rectify his mistake. By communicating with your youngster at the feeling level, you are teaching your child to be a sensitive person who cares for other people's feelings.

Another way to deal with your toddler is by "natural consequences." If he does not want to eat, he will be hungry. If he does not want to wear shoes to go outside, his feet may be hurt. If he steps on the toys, the toys may break, and he will not have the toys to play with anymore. If he does not learn to pick up his toys and you have to pick them up for him, you may put them away so that he will not be able to find the toys when he wants to play with them. All these are natural consequences that your child can learn to accept. By utilizing natural consequences, you are teaching responsibility, self-reliance, and self-confidence to your toddler.

Play with your toddler creatively. You do not need to have a lot of toys. More importantly, your toddler wants your companionship and your patience. Be patient with your toddler. Play with and teach your child. Colors, numbers, sizes, shapes, alphabets, and scribbling with a crayon or a marker are fun activities with your toddler. Be reminded that your youngster still has a very short attention span, typically no more than three to five minutes. For both of you to enjoy playing, you need to keep changing topics, taking the lead, and remaining in control; otherwise, your youngster will become disinterested, bored, and will wander away.

Reading books is no different. Short phrases, small paragraphs, and brief comments are typical for this age group. That is why Dr. Seuss' books are popular with toddlers. Expensive toys are of no use at this age. Your toddler will not appreciate them and will play roughly with them. Your toddler needs you. You need to be patient and devote plenty of time to your child. Make time for him. Remember, it was you who wanted to have children. You need to give him time and enjoy him as much as he enjoys you.

Keep your play and teaching simple. Otherwise, with all your good intentions, your toddler may be frustrated by all the failed attempts, hurting his ego. Achievable goals build confidence whereas repeated failures perpetuate frustration. Take little steps, steps you know your toddler can achieve to make it fun. Make your child feel good about himself. This will help your child build a positive self-image which will create good self-esteem that will be very useful in his teenage years. However, it is absolutely all right to let your toddler learn to tolerate frustration. After all, all of us will have frustrating moments in our lives. No one can protect us from them. Learning to tolerate and work with one's frustration is an important life goal we need to master early in our lives. You need to teach your youngster not to be afraid of frustration, but rather to deal with frustration patiently and effectively to overcome difficulties and develop problem-solving skills.

Your toddler finds eating fun. Your child will insist on self-feeding. He may be able to handle utensils like spoons and the forks well; however, sitting down to eat is another story. Since a two-year-old's attention span is still fairly short, it is all right for him to eat for a few minutes, go and play, then come back for a few more bites. A balanced diet is very important. You may need to keep a record of what your child has eaten and supplement that with what he may not have eaten in a day or so. Small, frequent feeding is still the key to a successful meal time. Remember, meal time should be a fun time for both of you!

Developmentally, your two-year-old can run fairly well and seldom falls. He can walk up and down the stairs by himself holding on to the side rail with your supervision. He can kick a large beach ball. He can turn pages of a book singly. He will probably insist that you read books to him. His fine motor movements are more mature, and he can build a tower of six to seven blocks before it falls. He loves to draw with crayons and markers, imitating vertical and circular strokes. He understands orders and can carry out your instructions precisely. He can speak two to three word phrases and has a vocabulary of around thirty words. He is starting to use pronouns. He may be able to pull simple garments on and off. He can indicate toilet needs to you or may already be toilet trained.

Your child should initiate toilet training by modeling you. It should be on his agenda, not anyone else's. After all, he is the only person who has all the control. If you alienate him at this task, you will find that you may lose the battle. You can scream, yell, and be frustrated, but if he does not want to use the toilet, there's nothing much you can do about it. You just cannot force his bowel or bladder to work. Neither can you help him to empty his bowel or bladder. You can, however, facilitate his desire to use the bathroom by inviting him to go with you when you need to use the rest-room. By demonstrating this repeatedly, he will get the idea and ask for a trial. If he is successful, all the better - praise him. If not, do not get frustrated - who promised us the first trial of anything would be successful? Be patient. Remember, about 50% of toddlers are not completely toilet trained by three years of age, particularly at night. Toilet training should be fun and without tears.

The physical examination will proceed next in the usual manner. Your doctor may want your toddler to sit on your lap for the examination. Or, if the youngster is ready, your doctor may want him to lie on the examination table. It all depends on what your toddler prefers. Most pediatricians can perform an adequate comprehensive physical examination while your toddler is sitting on your lap. Starting with the diaper area, one checks for the femoral pulses, inguinal hernias, lymph gland enlargement in the groin areas, undescended testis in boys and labial adhesions in girls. Next will be the inspection of the head and neck region, looking at the scalp, hair quality, facial area, the eyes, the nose, palpating the neck glands, checking for eczema behind the ears, and whispering to the youngster to check for hearing accuracy and response.

Then your doctor may auscultate the heart and the lungs - detecting any abnormal heart sounds and evaluating the quality of breath sounds and air entry to the lungs. Your doctor will palpate the abdomen to see if there is any abnormal enlargement of the abdominal organs. Next, your doctor will examine the mouth, inspecting the teeth, throat, and tongue, checking for obvious dental cavities, mal-occlusions, tongue thrust and abnormal enlargement of the tonsils. Finally, your doctor will need your help to examine the ear drums by holding your child's head steady. Do not be alarmed if your doctor detects an abnormality. After all, your doctor is the professional, trained to detect any problems your toddler may have.

While you are putting clothes on your toddler after the examination, your doctor may continue to discuss different issues with you, particularly injury prevention and self-comforting behaviors as age-appropriate ways of handling tension and stress. One cannot overemphasize the importance of injury prevention. A toddler is injury-prone. Your toddler needs to be supervised at all times, be it inside the house, out in the yard, or on the sidewalk. You just cannot leave your toddler alone. Shouting "no" has no meaning to a two-year-old. Toddlers do not understand or appreciate danger and are not ready to comply with your demands.

Do not leave your toddler alone in the car whether it is running or not. A child may accidentally release the parking brake, and the car may roll. Use car restraints consistently. Make it a habit that you will not start the car without every child being secured, either in the car seat or the seat-belts. This also applies to you and your adult companions. Guard against falls. Remove chairs and stepping-stools from areas where your toddler may climb to a dangerously high place. Ensure stair and window safety. Never leave a toddler unattended near a swimming pool, a bathtub full of water, or even a puddle of water - your toddler invariably wants to play in the water. Your toddler needs constant supervision.

Your doctor may discuss normal behaviors you should allow your toddler to perform, such as sucking a thumb or a pacifier, masturbation, using a transitional object such as a toy, a teddy bear or a blanket (be sure that you have two identical blankets, so that one can be washed without a fight). These are normal self-comforting behaviors to release stress and tension for your toddler. Parents should permit these. You may want to instruct your child to go to his room when he is masturbating, telling him that this should be performed in a private place. Without much interference, thumb-sucking and the use of a pacifier will stop before the age of four and should not have any bad, permanent effects on the teeth or cause mal-occlusion.

Enjoy your two-year-old. Play with him. Read to him. Encourage your child to "pretend" to stretch his imagination. Sing to him. Teach him songs that he can sing and enjoy. Let him talk. Teach him his name and his age. Help him learn to explore his surroundings. Take him outside in a small wagon. Let him walk. Your child appreciates your attention and your love. He learns to love and respect you as a caring, tender person!

Vaccinations need to be up-dated if any of the scheduled vaccinations have been missed. In most parts of United States, it is recommended to have the Hepatitis A vaccination. It is a series of two shots, six months apart. It should be given at two years of age with the second dose six months later. If the conjugated Pneumococcal vaccine was not given in infancy, the 23-valence Pneumococcal vaccine should be given after the age of two.

In summary, you may find that this visit is quite overwhelming. If you have further questions that need clarification, you may want to schedule another session to discuss specific issues that were not covered during the visit. You may want to talk with your spouse about the issues raised here and return for another consultation with your doctor. Or your doctor may refer you to other professionals, such as a clinical psychologist, a child psychiatrist, or a counselor for further evaluation and discussion.

Your doctor may suggest a time for the next checkup appointment, usually within the next year or so, depending upon your response during the visit. As you leave the doctor's office, armed with new insight about your toddler, you wonder what may come next as your youngster grows.

The Preschooler:
The Three- to Five-Year-Old

In general, the preschool years include children from three to five years of age. The common characteristics of this age group include the emergence of morality, the development of expressive language, the maturation of self-control, and the readiness for the entrance to formal education by five years of age.

You'll find that by now you are rarely seen in your pediatrician's office. For a change, your youngster is seldom sick. You may want to continue the yearly check-up by the pediatrician, or you may accumulate questions and make appropriate appointments for counseling or conferences with your doctor. The American Academy of Pediatrics still recommends annual check-ups until the age of six, then annually or bi-annually until maturity. The purpose for well-checks is to provide anticipatory guidance to both parents and youngsters and to conduct periodic examinations to check for the development of silent pathological processes that may require a physician's skill to detect. Routine tests may be performed and supervision of immunization status of the youngster will be monitored.

Your preschooler is a bundle of fun. Your child is innocent, always ready to ask questions whether you are ready for those questions or not. Be patient with your preschooler. A three-year-old youngster asks many questions every day. Every time you turn around there is a "why" or "how come," followed by "what's that," etc. This is the moment your youngster wants to learn and is most attentive to your teaching.

It is a great opportunity for you to teach your child. Be patient with your child. Just like any person, the first few explanations may not be adequate and your patience is important. Treat every question as an important question, and try your best to answer it. However, it is all right to admit that you do not know, but that you can help to find the answer for your child. Suggestions like, "We can go and ask daddy," or "We can go and find out at the library," are most appropriate, since this will teach your youngster how to find and learn new information. Most of all, you are teaching your youngster that no one knows everything. There is always room to learn. This will preserve your child's curiosity and inquisitiveness.

Try to avoid answers like "just because," "hush," and "wait a minute." These pacifying answers interrupt the learning opportunity for your youngster. Worst of all, they teach the youngster procrastination - to not solve problems as they come. More importantly, if your child gets only pacifying answers, he will be left alone to explore, possibly getting the wrong answers or getting into difficulties. In addition, these answers discourage learning. When you ask a teacher a question six or seven times and you only get pacifying answers, you will become very discouraged and not want to learn that subject anymore.

Be age appropriate with your answers. Put yourself at the level of your youngster. Try your best to explain to your child. Always try to give factually correct answers that can be understood. Your honesty will pay off in the long run. You will find that the same question comes up again and again, but if you give the facts, you will not need to remember what you said last time. Otherwise, your youngster may remember and get confused. Also, by demonstrating honesty and integrity, your youngster will learn these good virtues as time goes by. Your preschool child models you. He will learn your non-verbal communication skills as well. Your child will learn that what you teach him may not be the same as what you may do under certain circumstances. Be consistent.

A typical three-year-old child can go upstairs alternating feet. He enjoys the slide in the park. He can jump from the bottom step. Jumping is fun. Instead of pushing a tricycle with his feet, now he can pedal a tricycle. Tricycles, big-wheels, and other pedaling toys are enjoyments for a three-year-old. His fine motor development matures to a degree that he can write with a crayon, not scribbling anymore. He can copy circles and imitate making a cross. He can stack a tower of nine to ten cubes and tries to build a bridge with three cubes. He likes to read books, describing the pictures and the actions in picture books. He masters putting on shoes (simple ones without ties), and unbuttons buttons. He understands names and gender, follows commands, and can appreciate taking turns. He can feed himself well.

A typical four-year-old child can walk downstairs alternating feet. He can broad jump. He can throw a ball overhead and attempt to catch it. He can draw a human figure with two parts and can copy a cross. He can count to three correctly and can name one or more colors correctly. He can self-care, washing and drying his face and hands, brushing his teeth, and attempting to dress. He can cooperate by following commands and may even be able to do little errands with supervision like the setting dinner table, picking up toys, and working with parents or caretakers.

A five-year-old can skip, alternating feet. He can stand on one foot for more than eight seconds. He can draw an unmistakable human being with body parts, like hands, feet, body etc. He can copy a triangle and build two steps with cubes. He can count to ten without a mistake. He knows the four basic colors. He can describe actions in a picture book and enjoy reading with parents or accompanying adults. He may start asking for meanings of words and start to print a few letters. He can carry out three missions simultaneously. He can dress and undress without assistance. He has an attention span of about thirty to forty-five minutes. He can sit through a television show with an accompanying adult. He is ready for kindergarten now.

During the preschool stage, the family can now have a family meal. Mealtime is not as hectic as during the toddler years. A three-year-old child self-feeds well with spoon and fork. A four or five-year-old child can be expected to learn table manners with the basic skills of carefully handling the utensils to waiting for his turn during the meal. It should be fun to eat with your preschooler. If you still have toddlers in the family, you should start to take your preschooler out to eat in fancy restaurants, teaching him how adults enjoy food and giving your child an opportunity to practice the table manners he has learned. Otherwise, your child may not be able to understand why the toddler is allowed to have a bite then play whereas your preschooler needs to sit still and eat the meal.

This is also an opportunity to teach your youngster to eat a balanced diet. By putting all four food groups on the plate in small, child-size portions, your child is expected to eat all four food groups. If, for any reason, your child cannot finish the food on the plate, you should put the food in the refrigerator and save it for the next meal. Keep offering the food until the plate is emptied before offering new food items. This will ensure all four food groups are consumed. At the same time, this teaches your child that food is not to be wasted. This rule should, however, be applied to the entire household. Otherwise, your youngster will challenge you and ask why you can throw food away while he cannot. You may be tempted to eat the rest of the food on your child's plate. This is not advisable because no one should eat more calories than one needs, encouraging overeating with the associated morbidity and mortality of obesity. With time, your child will learn to take only the food that he can finish at one setting and will not try to overeat for any reason. For a three-year-old, snacks between meals are acceptable; however, as a child approaches five years of age, snacks should be discouraged. This is because you are trying to prepare your child for school where he will not have snacks between classes during the day.

As you walk in the office with your preschooler, the staff of the office will greet you. You will be advised to bring the youngster into the examination room and instructed to help undress your child down to his underwear to be weighed and measured. Weighing and measuring now will have the cooperation of your child. Thus, one can get fairly accurate measurements.

In a lot of pediatrician's offices, this is the first time your child's blood pressure will be taken. This may be a new experience for your child. Assure your child that this will not be painful. The office nurse will explain the procedure to your child. Some offices will also do a hearing and vision screen. These screening procedures will require the cooperation of your youngster. Not all pediatric offices do them as a routine office visit screenings. Of course, if your doctor finds something unusual, he or she may want to do either one or the other screen as indicated.

As your doctor comes into the examination room, he or she may note how well your youngster is growing, greeting your child as an individual, and, at the same time, greeting you and instructing you and your youngster to relax. If your doctor sees that your child is still rather apprehensive, he or she may console the youngster, explaining to your child that he can relax and that probably nothing extraordinary will happen to him. Your doctor may then address the conversation to the youngster, asking how he is doing, what things he likes to do and play with, and what chores your child does on a regular basis. By talking with your child, your doctor is trying to find out how your child feels about himself, how your child has adjusted to the family, his self-formation, and his self-image. Another important area is how your child feels towards any siblings, particularly younger ones. You can participate in the conversation, stating the facts and your true feelings in front of your doctor, making it important for your youngster to do the same. As you can see, this is the first opportunity your doctor may have to examine your child's psychological well-being, getting a handle on how your youngster thinks and feels about his psychosocial development.

Your doctor soon turns to you and asks whether you have any specific questions that you want to address. It is a good time for you to pour out any questions you may have, or you may let your doctor proceed with the normal procedure. Growth is an important issue on most parents' minds. Your doctor will address the question about growth by pointing out the normal growth curve he has been plotting since your child was a newborn. For a three-year-old, one may still measure the recumbent length rather than the standing height. Thus, there may be a noticeable shift when the way of measuring the height changes. Do not be alarmed. This is only a methodology fault. It has no meaning to the ultimate growth of your child.

Nutritional status may be assessed by the normal growth curve. If your doctor is sophisticated, he or she may want to measure the skin-fold thickness. This is a measure of the fatty tissue deposited on the skin, indirectly reflecting the amount of adipose tissue being formed in the body. Fat children grow to be fat adults. If your doctor is concerned about the excessive weight gain of your child, he or she may provide specific nutritional advice to you and your family. It is seldom necessary to put your child on a Weight Watchers diet. However, eliminating milk drinking (which is not essential at this age), avoiding certain types of snacks and deserts, cutting down on serving portions, and not encouraging compulsory emptying of the dinner plate may help develop good dietary habits for your youngster. It is important that the whole family follow the same principles; otherwise, your youngster will feel that he is being singled out for cruel and unusual punishment. The most common form of malnutrition in the United States of America is over-nutrition, and the population in America on the whole is being overfed. Over 60% of our population in the United States is considered over-weight! Overweight and obesity is of epidemic proportions in this country with all the complications that inflate our national health care costs! It is important to correct this trend early in life. A vitamin supplement is advisable, particularly one fortified with iron since food favoritism is common at this age. Calcium supplementation is also a good practice. Using the technique outlined at the beginning of this chapter helps to avoid food favoritism.

The physical examination proceeds as usual with the youngster lying on the examination table. For an apprehensive child, particularly for a three-year-old, an adequate examination can be performed on the parent's lap. However, your doctor normally prefers to examine the older ones lying on the examination table.

Your youngster may protest the examination of the external genitalia because of his modesty. However, this should be done particularly in girls since labial adhesion may still be a problem. You may not be bathing your child any more, and she may not realize that the labia should not be stuck together. The tendency of developing labial adhesion may last until your daughter reaches early puberty when the estrogen hormone begins to form in sufficient amounts to exert its effect on the external genitalia. Auscultation to the heart and lungs are done in the normal manner, as well as palpation of the abdomen, the hernial orifices, and the peripheral pulses. Reflexes are done and fundi are examined. A basic neurological examination may also be performed, along with checking hand-eye co-ordination, conjugation and eye movements, as well as examination of the cervical spine and the lumbar spine. Scoliosis is not a common finding at this age; however, one needs to establish the base line for future reference during the adolescent years.

Muscle strength may be assessed by asking the youngster to push and pull the examiner's arm so the full range of motion of the joints can be evaluated systematically. This examination may be fun for the youngster, especially if the doctor has established a good rapport with the child.

As your child starts to put on his clothes after the examination, your doctor may want to point out the positive findings to you and discuss their implications. If there are no abnormal findings that really means you are doing a good job of nurturing your youngster. However, if there are any problems, you will be glad that you brought your child to the office for this routine examination.

The subjects for discussion during the preschool years are many. One cannot ignore safety issues; particularly if you find your child is very independent. Your child may not ask or let you know where he is at every moment. There may be no way for you to monitor your youngster twenty-four hours a day. Teach your child good habits like always holding mother's hand before crossing the road, always riding the tricycle on the side-walk, and waiting and walking with mother or father to avoid accidents. Child-proofing your home is easier said than done at this age. Yet, you need to keep dangerous items like matches, firearms, knives, and heavy glass ornaments away from your child since they may be dangerous to the child as well as to other people. Lock these items in a safe place. Remember, your preschooler is curious and will copy whatever you may do even though this is not what you intend to teach your child.

As a three-year-old child learns the concept of right from wrong, good from bad, sequence and consequence, the guardian may need to let him learn in actual practice with supervision. Obviously, no one would want a three -year-old endangering himself, yet the "natural consequence" lessons are important lessons. Statements like "if you do not eat, you will be hungry;" "if you do not pick up your toys and we pick them up, you may not be able to find them when you need them," "if you do not wear shoes to go outside, your feet may be hurt" and "if you touch the stove, your fingers may be burned," are examples of natural consequences. No one, not even mother or father, can change the consequences. One just needs to learn these lessons from one's experiences in life! Through these natural consequences, your youngster learns to be a responsible person. At the same time, he learns that he can control the outcome of his actions. This empowerment is very important for the development of his self-image. He learns he can control his destiny, if he desires, in his own environment.

For an unruly three-year-old, parents need to be able to enforce certain rules for him to learn. Just words may not be enough. One needs to be firm and act consistently, but not necessarily raising one's tone of voice in anger. Parents need to carry out what they say with the appropriate action to back up their reasoning so the message to the youngster is loud and clear. There should be no confusion about the message. "Time-out" can be an effective method to contain a three-year-old, but one needs to appreciate the limitations of this method. Otherwise, it becomes ineffective. You need to be calm, in control, and be age appropriate. You can state why you want to have a time-out so that your youngster understands what has happened and can avoid this next time. However, "time-out" will not work well without a "time-in" period. "Time-ins" are periods of positive interaction with you or your spouse. Your youngster longs for and enjoys "time-ins."

Personal hygiene can be taught by four years of age. Sure enough, good habits as well as bad habits are formed the same way. If your child is taught to wash hands before each mealtime, your child will learn to do so without being reminded in due time. Similarly, brushing teeth, bathing, grooming, self-caring, and being punctual for mealtimes or any social functions are important habits for your child to learn early in life. Your child requires your supervision, yet he can learn to be responsible for his decisions.

Parents want their children to be obedient. Yet, assertiveness is a much more important quality than obedience alone. Your youngster needs to learn reasoning and consequences instead of blind obedience. Unfortunately, in our society, there are plenty of people who may exploit our children making simple obedience dangerous to them. Yet, teaching them to be assertive requires the child to think about what is appropriate and what may be good for him, as an individual or as a group, so that he can voice his concerns under any situation. This kind of training requires very understanding parents who truly treat their child as an equal individual, so that they can have meaningful discussions on any subjects that may arise in the course of every day life. Of course, the parent, being the ultimate responsible party, should have the final voice on any decision making, with the appropriate reasoning to support their arguments. This will teach the democratic process to our children so that they are not afraid to speak up for their own rights. After all, we are trying to teach them to thrive and survive in our democratic society.

Teaching children the concept of respect is an important aspect of development. Respect is mutual. You need to respect your child's ideas before your child learns to respect yours. Your child is as much an individual as you are. You can use reasoning and simple logic to explain to your youngster so that he will understand your point of view. By maintaining control of yourself, you will find that your child will learn to respect your arguments without you needing to raise your voice or be violent. By demonstrating this kind of self-control, your child will learn to appreciate your respect for him. Soon, your child will be able to maintain a normal tone of voice to discuss any issue with you in the future.

Respecting others and self-respect are two very important qualities your child needs to achieve before formal education begins. Your child's teacher deserves respect from his or her pupils; simultaneously, you want his peers as well as the teaching staff to respect your child. It is essential that you introduce such concepts at home during the formative years. Otherwise, your child will be left with a bruised ego in the early days of schooling. This might interfere with your child's future.

The concept of love is important for a preschooler. Obviously, he will love his parent, siblings, friends, and relatives. The same concept needs to extend to animals and inanimate objects. Behavior like kicking the dog when he walks by just for fun is not an acceptable behavior. Throwing a toy down to see it break is similarly unacceptable. One should be able to extend one's love from human beings to animals and to inanimate objects. This concept of love is the basis for justice and equality. This teaches the youngster to be a sensitive person. Be nice to people, animals, and objects is an important concept for him to learn. He will be greatly rewarded when people observe his behavior, kindness, and serenity. This concept needs to be demonstrated by the parents to the child. Parents need to show children how to care for each other, how to be concerned when one does not feel well, and how to love one another. When the parents have disagreements, they can show the children how to solve their conflicts with civil discussions, debates, and arguments, maintaining respect for one another. By living the standard of what we preach, the child learns and models.

Communicate with your preschooler. Communicate with him on an emotional level. "How do you feel to-day?" and "How can mommy make you feel better?" are good, exploring, sensitive questions that you should ask your preschooler on a daily basis, particularly after you have been away for any period of time, such as after work or school. This will teach your youngster to be sensitive to your feelings, also. It is important for you to share your feelings with your youngster so that he may learn to appreciate how hard it is for you to provide and care for him. This kind of exercise will have an enormous impact on the future development of your relationship with your child. And, you may be building the foundation of open communication with your child for many years to come.

The emergence of morality in young children in itself is a big topic. However, there are basic theories one can follow. Kohlberg's six stages of moral development is one of the more popular examples to follow. As indicated before, from birth to about eighteen months of age, the youngster is considered "amoral," reflecting the fact that the toddler has no real concept of "right" and "wrong," "good" and "bad," and "acceptable" and "not acceptable." As children enter the first level of moral development at the pre-conventional state, toddlers learn to obey an order to avoid punishment. They learn that rules are provided by authorities and they focus on prevention of punishment and other unpleasant consequences. At stage two, still in the pre-conventional level, they realize that there are several facets to an issue, and they have the freedom to choose and bargain. Between the ages of three and five, children enter into the conventional level of moral development. At stage three of Kohlberg's moral development, children enter into peace making, negotiating, and maintaining harmony with other individuals. They consider "why" things are done in a certain way to maintain peace and tranquility. You can start to reason with them. It is at this stage of development that children are ready to enter formal schooling in society.

During the preschool years, another important task the youngster needs to master is self-discipline. By modeling parents, this principle is basically acquired at home. The child needs to learn that none of us get what we want all the time. We need to learn "give and take" techniques to survive in our society. When Junior does not want to go to the day-care center today, it does not necessarily mean that mother or father will not go to work and stay home to play with Junior. Of course, most of us would rather be with our youngster than go to work; yet we all know better. This is self-discipline. The youngster will soon learn that it is useless to throw a temper tantrum, screaming and kicking. The child will still have to go to the "day-care" center. However, parents do not need to be frustrated for it is through these protests that the youngster learns how well your self-discipline works and how firmly you stand on your principles.

Learn to work with your preschooler. He is eager to work. He wants to learn. Enlist him in a few simple household chores. He may not be perfect the first few times he tries, but none of us are. Let him learn, let him gain experience and enjoy working. By lessening your chores, you may have more quality time to spend with him and enjoy him.

Encourage your child to play with other children. He will learn the value of sharing and friendship. He will learn "give and take;" he will learn how to negotiate. Be sure to supervise the children's play, but try not to intervene when they quarrel or fight unless danger exists. Let natural consequences work. You may have to provide explanations to him, on his level, so that he will learn and appreciate your efforts of letting him make decisions.

Read to your preschooler, bring him to libraries and reading clubs. He will learn to enjoy reading for the rest of his life.

You do not need to get angry when he tries to push you to the limit. Loosing your temper just shows your youngster that you do not have self-control. Be firm, but gentle. Reassure your child. When you leave your child at day care centers or church groups, let your child know that you will come and pick him up on time, every time. And, tell him that you love him and miss him as much as he misses you. This message of love will come through loud and clear to the youngster. With time, he will understand that you are a person of integrity and principles. He will learn not to manipulate you. At the same time, he will learn from your examples of self-discipline and self-determination which will benefit him for life.

Finally, your doctor may point out that your youngster should have a booster dose for diphtheria, tetanus, pertussis, poliomyelitis, measles, mumps, rubella and conjugated hemophilus influenza vaccines, as well as a tuberculosis skin test before the start of the formal school years.

The Six- To Nine-Year-Old

As your child enters formal schooling, he emerges into a new society where children from different backgrounds, different ethnic groups, and different social and economic environments merge together under the guidance of a teacher. The teacher becomes the new authority figure in your child's mind. You may find your youngster running towards you, yelling "Mommy, mommy, you don't know! Ms. So and So taught me this today!" You will find that mother and father do not always know the answers, no matter what your educational background is. This is all right. This means that you are no longer the ultimate authority in the eyes of your child. The teacher is. You need to cooperate with the teacher. The teacher has good intentions for your child. Teachers are there to teach your child and, with your permission, to mold your child into a mature human being in the forthcoming years. The teacher will have a long, lasting impression on your child. Please try to work with the teacher. If you have to contradict the teacher for any reason, the best way to do it is through a parent-teacher conference, or simply by booking an appointment with the teacher to share your point of view. Please do not contradict the teacher in front of your child. You will cause confusion in your child's mind, shaking his confidence in this new authority, and creating a future hardship for your child in school.

A report card is an important document. You should bring a copy with you when you take your child to the doctor's office for his appointment. Your pediatrician may have a different interpretation on what he or she sees in the report card. Grades are not important - learning is. It is much more important for your child to master the concepts that are taught, rather than just get a good grade.

Learning should be fun for your child. He should feel the challenge and be stimulated to learn the new concepts and new insights that are taught to him on a daily basis. You should provide a good, quiet place for your child to learn, do homework, and prepare lessons for the next day. You do not need to answer any questions for your child. That is the teacher's job. Your job is to nurture the child. Play the parent's role at home and try not to be the teacher. If your child does not understand a certain concept, it is his responsibility to ask the teacher and to pay attention at school. If you keep on bailing him out at home by doing his homework or teaching him at home, you are empowering him not to learn at school. After all, most children like to interact with their parents. They can easily con you into being their teacher so that they do not need to pay attention in school. Worst of all, your child may then be labeled "hyperactive" with a "short attention span," and get negative attention rather than havng a positive experience in school.

Leave the teaching job to the teachers. Be supportive of the teachers. By providing a nurturing, learning environment at home, your child will be able to learn. You can, however, supplement learning by providing opportunities to broaden your child's horizon, such as going to the library on a regular basis, going to the zoo, the park, or the museum, where he can have fun and learn at the same time. After all, learning should be a lifetime process. One can learn from any teacher, in any place, and at any time. Learning is a continual process. Learning is for all of us.

Expect your children to learn good things as well as bad things at school. After all, just like a miniature society, you will find good qualities being taught by the teachers, yet your youngster may learn bad things from other children with different backgrounds. Accept this. This is not the teacher's fault. You should be able to stop this by correcting your youngster, explaining your reasoning and your concerns. You may also report this to the teacher, and always with an open mind, not to incriminate the teacher's intent. After all, no teacher can be with all the children at all times of the day. Children learn bad words, bad behaviors, and bad habits at school. It is your responsibility to tell the teacher your concerns so that the teacher can direct his effort to curtail the spread of such behavior in the classroom. Do not blame the teacher. The teacher is only a sub-contractor, helping you teach your child under your local authority to establish a certain standard for your child. Your caring attitude and cooperation will be appreciated.

When you call the pediatrician's office for an appointment, you must let the office staff know the specific purpose of the appointment. For a well child visit at this age, the office staff may allocate more time for this particular visit dependent upon how frequently you bring your child in for such a visit, the specific questions you have, and the pediatrician's agenda for this age group. It also depends on whether there are any particular issues that the school may require, such as pre-participant sports evaluations, tests for hearing difficulties, vision problems, or inattentiveness and hyperactivity. Each of these issues requires a different focus. The office staff need to alert the physician ahead of time so that he or she can prepare for your questions and not waste your time and effort. Well checks at this age may be booked in advance, usually months ahead of the time, so please do make a note on your calendar to remind yourself. Sometimes, the physician's office may issue a reminder for you about a week before the visit to facilitate optimal use of the physician's time. Remember to bring along report cards, progress reports, and typical work of your child so your doctor can make an objective judgment of your child's performance.

Your child should feel comfortable walking into the doctor's office. Your child may still be a little anxious, but not really frightened and or resistant. The office staff will welcome you and update some demographic information, and instruct you and your child to enter the examination room. Some nine-year-olds may be modest, unwilling to undress for weighing and measuring. However, most doctors' offices are equipped with gowns that may be used for such a purpose. Please do not hesitate to ask the receptionist or the office nurse to provide some privacy to ensure your child's comfort and cooperation. If the positive relationship has been previously established, it will not be difficult for you and your child to be at ease and ready for the examination.

As weight and height are plotted on the growth curves, you and your child will find out how well he has been growing. Your child may be concerned about the weight gained in previous years. Or, you may be concerned that your child has not gained much weight at all. Normally, there is no need for concern. Children grow differently. Some girls may already be at early puberty, while others may still be in the latency period. Let your doctor make the interpretation. Your doctor is trained for it. Blood pressure will be obtained, sometimes in both sitting and recumbent positions. Some doctor's offices routinely screen for hearing deficit and visual acuity, depending on the prevalence of these disorders in the community. Some offices also screen for urinary tract infection and nutritional anemia on a routine basis. It all depends on what your doctor believes about these issues. Universal serum lead screening for children is not advisable because it is expensive, difficult to interpret the results, and impossible to resolve the social issues surrounding lead poisoning. However, your doctor may still elect to perform the test, particularly if there are symptoms suggestive of chronic lead exposure.

When obtaining the interval history, your pediatrician may ask whether there are any specific concerns you want to discuss about growth and nutrition or school performance. Your doctor starts to observe the interaction between you and your child, with particular reference to the emotional exchange during the questions and answers.

Your doctor may deliberately engage in conversation with your child to see how your child feels, thinks, and acts to specific questions regarding his well-being. The questions may concern school, home, playgrounds, friends or relatives. You should take notes on those responses that alarm or surprise you to further discuss in this visit or at a subsequent visit.

The physical examination will be performed in the usual manner, dependent on the purpose of this visit. If this is a sport's physical, your doctor may try to exert your youngster a little, moving all the joints of the extremities and testing for muscle strength. Examination of the cardiovascular system may require a little more time, with emphasis on the cardiac reserve, peripheral pulses, blood pressure on supine and recumbent positions, as well as on all four extremities. Simple neurological examination is performed to test for hand/eye coordination, eye muscle movement, balance, deep tendon reflexes, joint mobility, muscle strength, cutaneous sensations, and scoliosis. Dental hygiene is an important issue. By six years of age, the first permanent molar may start to erupt and the front deciduous teeth may be loose or shed. Appropriate dental referral should be made if the youngster still does not have routine dental care. Assessment of sexual maturity may also be made if your young girl is starting to show breast-budding by nine years of age. Your doctor will then start another phase of the examination, instructing your youngster to dress.

Developmentally, your six-year-old is expected to be able to bounce a ball five to six times, pitch a ball, and catch it again. He is able to ride a bicycle without training wheels, follow simple traffic rules, and take all the safety precautions. He can skate or roller-blade. This activity requires adult supervision. On roller-blades, a child may achieve a speed up to twenty plus miles an hour. A crash accident may cause significant injury. He can stand on one foot with his eyes closed for more than ten seconds and maintain his balance. He can build three steps with building blocks. He can tie shoelaces and care for himself in the morning. He can get ready for school. He can differentiate morning from evening and knows his right hand from his left hand. He can do simple addition and subtraction. He can write his name and write numbers up to ten correctly. He can draw a man with six body parts, including clothes.

By seven years of age, your child is expected to be fairly independent. He can get up in the morning and get ready for school. He can be expected to take care of his homework and his belongings, both at school and at home. He can enjoy reading simple stories and watching television independently, with an attention span of about 45 minutes. He can participate in household chores and care for younger siblings. He can maintain friends and playmates. He is socially active.

By eight years of age, he develops a sense of humor. He can make jokes and laugh about them. He is able to tell time and is responsible for keeping time. He now reads for pleasure and can maintain a library card. He learns to respect the property of other people and is responsible for what he does, at home, in school, and in other social environments. He learns to care about his appearance, both at home and in public. He learns to take good care of his belongings and picks up and cleans his bedroom.

By nine years of age, most children can master the daily activities at home and at school independently. They can prepare simple meals like breakfast or snacks and understand the nutritional needs of an individual. They can participate in group activities, helping to maintain harmony with family and peers. They know what is expected of them in certain settings, and they can perform their duties. They can freely express their opinion when they are asked. They know the rules and morals of the family. They are setting the stage for early adolescence.

During the latency stage of childhood development, your child may not show many changes. This, in fact, is a maturation period. Your child assembled all the information he gathered during the formative years with all the self and moral development, applied it in a school setting to test his skill in handling the information. You may find that your talkative preschooler has turned into a quiet person, with limited, simple answers when your doctor tries to converse with him. This is normal. The reserve he shows is a reflection of his self awareness. Your child enters into the concrete operational stage of development, able to perform mental calculations in his mind and develop rules to govern his own experience. Morally, he can maintain social order and be a good citizen, understanding the functions of the rules, not just the existence of the rules. He can now appreciate the logic of different operations and can relate sequence of events by simple logic. Logical consequence is another powerful tool that parents may want to learn and utilize as an important armament in teaching and disciplining the child.

Self-concepts are maturing. Your youngster will appreciate your trust in him, be it under your direct guidance or when he is alone. You will find that self-governing is an important concept for both you and your youngster to master. You should be able to empower your youngster to make decisions, to test his judgment, and see the results of his work. Self-motivation is one of the most important qualities in life that we can teach our children. He can appreciate the need when you want him to help without you asking him to do so. He should be able to clean and tidy his room before leaving for school in the morning. He should be solely responsible for work at school and his homework. He should be able to defer gratification until the tasks are done.

Natural consequence is still a good technique for parents to utilize in order for the youngster to learn to master self-motivation. Parents should not need to go in the youngster's room to clean up the mess. It is his responsibility to see that if his room is not picked up, the time lost trying to find things in the room is his loss. Be reasonable. If your youngster asks you to help, of course, you are more than happy to help clean. But, refrain from offering to help if it is not at his request. Otherwise, natural consequences will not work, and you may just be his maid for the next ten years. Common ground requires common efforts. It is all right for all the family members to participate in cleaning up the den after a party or for everybody to take part in cleaning the yard after the winter months, preparing for spring. This also means that parents need to take part, too. If you just sit there and order your children around, you are being a bad example and inviting resentment. Always remember that you are a role model for your child. Your actions speak a lot louder than your words as far as your child is concerned.

"Grandmother's Rule" is a good rule. It means that one should always finish working before play time. This simple rule should be applied fairly to every member of the family. This will stop procrastination since the earlier the work is done; the earlier one gets to play. At the same time, if the work is not done properly, then the natural consequence will be more corrections and further deferment of play activities.

Your youngster requires recognition and support. You need to show your appreciation for his cooperation. As time allows, you should invite him to little parties to show your approval and that you are proud of him. If things at home are clean and tidy, you and your child will have more time to enjoy each other, again, as a consequence of his cooperation. By nurturing your youngster during the latency years, you are laying the foundation for the forthcoming adolescent and teenage years, when you may find parenting is a lot more challenging and complex than before.

Your doctor may ask if you have any questions or concerns that you want to address. He or she may suggest reading materials for you and your spouse concerning parenting techniques and styles. Or, your doctor may make a referral to sub-specialists in child development or child psychology.

As you leave the doctor's office with new insight on working with your youngster, you find that this office visit was well worth your time and effort.

The Early Adolescent Years

By the early adolescent years, you may be bringing your children to the pediatrician's office mainly for a sport physical on an annual or bi-annual basis. However, this is a very important stage in your child's development. You may find that you need guidance and support on different issues in parenting, including study habits, work ethics, respect of parents, getting along with siblings and peers, participation in group activities, and most of all, the self-development during these critical years of transition from childhood to adulthood status.

The early adolescent years are characterized by the growing awareness of emerging self-development. The young adolescent tries to find his position at home, in school, with friends, at church and in society. Your child is becoming more aware of his appearance and may spend hours in the bathroom, preparing for any function, even for daily activities like going to school. Your child will be offended if you criticize the time spent on such chores like bathing, grooming, dressing, and putting on make-up. From the familiar "Mommy, you don't know" to "Mommy, you don't understand," it is really a big step forward for the youngster, since these words reflect the feeling of the growing adolescent towards adult guardians. Accept your child. Your child is growing up and needs to learn to make decisions. All the fundamental principles that you may have laid down in prior years are now put to the test. Your adolescent child is beginning to challenge the rules that you have instituted in the family for many years, and he may start to make his own judgments and interpretations.

By accepting your youngster, you are providing room for discussion and nurturing; otherwise, you may be unwillingly forcing your child to rebel, run away from home, or do things much worse than you can ever imagine. This is totally unnecessary. You can guide your child; however, you cannot live for your child nor can you follow your child twenty-four hours a day, seven days a week. By empowering your child to be his own guardian, you suddenly shift the responsibility of guardianship to your child. Be sure to let your child know that you will always be there to consult before he has to make an important decision. You can have a civil discussion and let your child make the final decision, provided it does not affect his safety, the safety of the family, or society. Accepting this responsibility, your child will feel mature, trusted, and most of all, grown up.

The liberty of decision-making is always followed by the consequence of the decision. Your child is responsible for the consequence that comes with his decision. This may sound scary for a lot of parents; however, if you think for a minute, it only makes good sense. As you cannot follow your child all the time, at some point he will have to make decisions independently. Moreover, if you do not let him bear the consequence of his decision-making, you will deprive him of learning opportunities to refine his decision-making skills. All of us make good and bad decisions. We all learn from the consequences of our bad decisions. If we do not let our youngster learn and bear the consequence of his bad decision, the youngster will be ill-prepared for the future where no one can bail him out all the time. He has to learn early that he must be willing to see the consequence of his decision and be responsible for it. You, as a caring parent, can advise him when you are consulted. Most of the time, your spontaneous suggestions will only make things worse unless your youngster has a great rapport with you. Accept your child. Out there in this world, things can get much worst! Do not force your youngster to jump the fence and run away from home. Home is where your child belongs.

Early Adolescent Girls

Normally, girls mature a little earlier than boys. By ten years of age, most girls are in their early pubertal development. You will find that your innocent little girl suddenly becomes shy and self-aware, spending more and more time in the bathroom in the mornings getting ready for school. You may receive telephone calls day and night, asking for your daughter instead of you or your spouse. Times have changed. She is moving towards a new stage of development that is very important for you and your child. By handling this stage well, you will find joy, peace, and tranquility with your daughter. On the other hand, you will have years of sorrow, regret, and disappointment about your dreams for your little princess if you fail at this stage.

Before any physical indication of puberty, suddenly you find your daughter becomes moody, difficult to please, often critical of your normal behavior (at least what you thought was "normal behavior"), and always ready for a debate or fight with either one of you. Typically, she has an explanation for everything and anything, she knows everything, and any of your comments, whatever your intent, are stupid and dumb. She has no use for your suggestions and comments. She can also be very manipulative. When she needs a favor from you, she will see to it that you either give in or are ready for another fight, with tears, screaming, and the normal temper tantrums you may have forgotten during the latency years. You want your innocent little girl back. Mood swings are typical for the early adolescent girl. Get prepared. You will be able to survive the next few years.

Because of the awareness of the changing self, most early adolescent girls refuse to go to the doctor unless there is a specific reason for them to do so. Typically, she wants to be in a certain sport that requires a pre-participation physical examination, or the family has set a routine for the annual physical, usually at the beginning of summer vacation. If your visit is specifically for a sports physical, please let the physician's office staff know so that time is allowed and the examination will not be hurried. The discussion preparing for the teen years may take up to forty-five minutes of time, particularly if you or your daughter have questions that are not covered by your doctor's discussion. Again, always make a list of the questions you want to cover so that you will make the best use of your time and your doctor's time. Interviewing the family is almost always done with parents and daughters sitting down together in the same examination room; however, it is not unusual for the parent to be asked to leave the room during the examination, particularly if the father comes with his daughter. Most offices have female nursing staff available if the girl does not feel comfortable with a male doctor.

Routine measurements are made by the office nurse, including weight, height, blood pressure, vital signs, sometimes skin fold thickness, vision acuity and hearing screening. All of these are recorded as usual. Your doctor may prefer that the youngster wear a gown during the examination, or some doctors may let her wear a top for the examination. Other than a general physical examination, your doctor may focus on several areas of special concern, unlike the previous examinations. Skin is a big topic for girls of this age, particularly acne and skin care. With the current popularity of sun-tanning, one also needs to discuss sun-injury to the skin including the use of sun-block to prevent skin cancer. Puberty thyroid gland enlargement is common in girls. The thyroid glands are palpated for enlargement, auscultated for bruit, and evidence of hyper- or hypothyroidism is assessed. Examination of the spine is important since most idiopathic scoliosis develops at this age. It is not uncommon to teach parents to examine the daughter's spine on a regular basis, once every three months or so. The curvature is important and so is the rib hump. The parents should be aware of the development of the spine to detect the early deviation from normal and seek appropriate remedial exercise and therapy.

Last but not the least, is the examination of the secondary sexual organ development. Tanner staging is an accepted standard by most authorities in the assessment of sexual maturation. The adolescent girl should be taught self-examination of her breasts and her external genitalia. This can be taught by viewing a film, by using a model, or both so that the youngster feels comfortable doing the examination on a monthly basis. If she should have any doubt about the examination, she should report this to her mother or her physician for reassurance and counseling.

A discussion of the growth curve is important for the adolescent girl as most girls think they are overweight at this age. We plot the weight for height curve which is an important comparison for the adolescent since she may not know that girls start puberty at very different ages. By just plotting the traditional growth curve, one may mislead the adolescent into thinking she is overweight for her norm and push her into unhealthy dieting, or even worse, to anorexia nervosa or bulimia. A good discussion on nutrition is important for the adolescent girl. Since her physical growth is going to accelerate, she will need more energy to cope with both the increased activity of physical growth and the loss in her menstrual flow. Supplemental vitamins, iron, and calcium are essential for the adolescent girl. The use of tampons should be discouraged, particularly super-absorbent tampons. They have been linked to toxic-shock syndrome, a highly fatal condition for otherwise normal girls. If the use of a tampon is not avoidable, the youngster should be taught to change her tampon every two hours whether she needs to or not. This is the only acceptable way to prevent toxic-shock syndrome. Prepare the youngster for menstrual periods. It may be very scary for the early adolescent girl caught unaware, particularly at camp or during physical education class. The first few periods are typically silent without much cramping or spotting. Teach her to accept the responsibility of being a girl. She will have to learn to manage this soon to be monthly affair for the next 35 to 40 years.

Early Adolescent Boys

On average, boys mature a little later than girls. Most boys reach early adolescence by twelve to fourteen years of age. It has been observed that boys also have mood swings in the early teens just as early adolescent girls do; however, they may not be as obvious as those for girls. A lot of boys have violent tempers at this stage of development. They tend to involve parents in fights that may not have happened just one year before. Because of their physical strength, it is not advisable for parents to engage in physical punishment at this age, even though physical punishment should not have any role in modern parenting. Violence breeds violence. In order for our society to curtail violence, it is crucial to start at home. Sports activities are important to boys, particularly during the early adolescent years. However, because of the different rates of reaching puberty, young adolescent boys may have difficulty competing with the more mature opponent, even though they are the same age. Boys are also more adventurous. They have more of a risk-taking behavior, and any unsupervised activity may turn into a disaster. However, they are also trying to establish their independence and their own identity. It is important for parents to remember that you cannot "baby" them any more. Natural consequences is a good tool for this particular age since they have mastered the concrete operational stage of development.

Again, most routine physical examinations for adolescent boys are for pre-participation sports evaluation. This should be scheduled ahead of time so that you will have adequate time to ask questions and your doctor will allow enough time for your youngster. Do not wait until the coach starts training sessions before you call and book the appointment. You are not being fair to your youngster or your doctor, and you will find that this visit is important for both of you.

The office staff takes routine measurements, as usual, recording the height, weight, blood pressure, vital signs, and optional visual screen and hearing screen. Most boys do not require a gown for the examination. Undressing the youngster to the underwear should be adequate if the patient is comfortable with this. Otherwise, a gown may be provided. He should receive the same respect as the adolescent girl. Most boys notice changes in their body, particularly their changing voice when they talk and their external genitalia. They may also be concerned about pimples and other eruptions on the skin. It is normal for boys to find that their breasts become tender and grow. This may alarm them, making them wonder what in the world is happening to them. They simply need reassurance. This may not be symmetrical; one breast may be more tender and swollen than the other. Avoiding undue stimulation of the breast tissue and the introduction of infection is the only precaution one needs to take for this condition.

The physical examination will proceed as normal, with particular attention paid to the muscular-skeletal system and the cardiovascular system. Mobility of all the joints and the grading of all muscle strength should be done in a systematic fashion. Sometimes, if there is any suggestion of exercise-induced bronchial spasm, exercise tolerance may have to be performed to assess the advisability for competitive sports. As for the cardiovascular system, other than auscultation, one needs to evaluate all the peripheral pulses, their quality, and their difference between extremities. One needs to evaluate blood pressure, comparing the supine and sitting, or standing blood pressures with the established normal standard for the age. Assessment of sexual maturity by the Tanner staging of the development of the testis, of the secondary sex characteristics, as well as the penis should be done. At this point, the youngster should be taught how to examine the testicles and how to clean the glans of the penis from smegma. Checking for the development of inguinal hernias, particularly for weight-lifting sports, is also important to remember. To a lesser degree, boys can also develop scoliosis, particularly tall boys. Teaching the parents to examine the spine may be important if the boy's predicted height is over six feet tall. This should be performed at home by the parents about every three to six months. Early detection and intervention of scoliosis may prevent further collapse of the spine which requires surgical intervention in the future. A general discussion of diet is also important for boys since they are going to grow at a rapid pace for the next few years. Your son needs to establish good eating habits with a balanced diet to prevent nutritional deficiencies and obesity. Multiple vitamins with iron and calcium supplementation may also be important for adolescent boys.

Topics of discussion may vary with each individual physician. It also depends on the agenda of the accompanying parents. The following topics are chosen because they are common concerns that easily create conflicts in the family. It is particularly important to have the foundation set for the next few years for both the early adolescent and the family.

Household Work

It may be hard to involve your early adolescent in household work without a lot of protest and fuss; however, as in any community living, one needs to participate and share the burden to feel needed. It is as important an educational experience as going to school. A youngster does not need to be told to do certain work. Your child should learn that communal grounds in the house require all members help to maintain. Natural consequences works wonders. Role modeling is also very important. If you start to work on household chores, your youngster normally will follow, since they learn to appreciate your efforts. You want to promote self-motivation rather than just ordering your child to do certain sets of chores. Ordering around your early adolescent calls for resentment and you are inviting fights with your children. However, by role modeling, you will find that your youngster eventually will learn to follow. Doing dishes, picking up, dusting, and even cooking dinner together can be fun for the family; it just depends on the attitude of the parties involved. With the individual's territory, like the bedroom, it should be up to the individual's choice and taste. Parents are advised not to march into the youngster's room and demand that he pick up everything and clean up immediately for inspection. Certain safety rules apply - food and eating utensils should not be in the bedroom, doorways should be clear in case of a fire - and can be outlined for the youngster to follow. Other than that, one can utilize the power of natural consequences to accomplish the desired results. For example, if the room is not picked up as you like, you will find that the person being inconvenienced is your child. The messier the room, the harder for the youngster to find whatever he may need for that moment; it is the consequence of your child's decision. If all the clothes are on the floor, your child will not have clean, presentable clothes to wear. Soon, your youngster will learn that you are not going to do all these chores for him and that he will have to do them.

Another advantage is that your child will learn to be a master of himself. It is true that when you first implement this, you will find that your youngster may protest by not picking up at all. However, after six months of inconvenience, he will learn that you are not his maid anymore, and if he decides not to clean his room, he will just have to live with the consequences of his decisions and actions. When the youngster sees the consequences and desires to do something about it, he may request help. It is all right to help when you are being asked; however, he has to participate and help with other projects in return. This way, the lesson can be learned. Otherwise, you may be unconsciously doing all the cleaning chores again.

A general rule is that when the youngster stops picking up or cleaning, it is time for you to stop as well. Working as a team is a lot more fun for both you and your child. You should always honor the privacy of your adolescent child. Even when you are requested to help clean the bedroom, if there are areas that your child wants to keep private, they should be left untouched. Once you violate the trust of your child, it may be a long time before your youngster trusts you again. Thus, whenever your child wants to leave the room, it is perfectly all right for you to leave as well. This way, your child knows that you will not violate your pledge of not cleaning for him, and at the same time, you let your child know that you honor his privacy. By early adolescence, your youngster should be taught to do their own laundry, particularly girls, since they may value their clothes and undergarments more than boys. They should be taught how to sort clothes and how to care for them by ironing, bleaching, and removing stains. Through these lessons, they will learn to be careful with their clothing by preserving them and avoiding stains.

Allowance

An allowance is important for your adolescent children. The allowance should be enough to cover the expenses of the week, plus a reasonable amount for pocket money and savings. This should be started as early as the sixth grade, when your youngster needs lunch money. Instead of giving your child the needed lunch money on a daily basis, you can sit down with him on Sunday evenings and distribute the allowance for the week. There are many advantages to this system. First, you are teaching your youngster to be responsible for the money. If your child is careless with his own money, he will learn that by lunch time the money will not be there, and he will have to go hungry. If he loses the money, it should not be replaced~the suffering is for that week. This will force the issue of responsibility on the youngster. You are also giving him the liberty to choose how to save and spend. If he spends all the money on Monday, he will be hungry for lunch for the rest of the week. If he spends more on one day, then on the next day he will have to spend less. This also teaches the youngster to learn to budget which will be important for the rest of his life.

The saving of money is also important. It has been shown that those children who grow up learning to save and defer their gratification are more successful as adults in society. This will also teach the child to be a wise, comparative shopper who knows the value of money. The allowance should be given to the youngster but not tied to the amount of work that he does in the household. An allowance is not a paycheck for household chores. An allowance is given as a token of love where parents see their children's needs and provide for them. In the capitalistic society of America, it is common to see that if the son does certain chores, the father or mother pays the child a certain sum of money as an allowance. This actually creates the social disaster we now face in America. When the parents grow old, unable to work, or do any chores for the grown children, the adult children will leave the old folks to the government, feeling no guilt for not supporting their old folks "since they are not working for me!" Love is mutual; feelings are mutual, also. If your children learn to appreciate how you try to provide for him without any conditions but love and respect, they learn to reciprocate in the years to come. It is only in America that we have a significant "old-age" problem. This can be solved if we plan ahead and plant the seed of mutual love and respect early in the adolescent's mind. The allowance should be adjusted as the adolescent matures, and the parents can let the youngster be responsible for more than just lunch money. After all, by the time your child is ready for college, he should be able to buy all the supplies, clothes, necessities, and pay for tuition, room and board, books and fees, etc. This is an important lesson for the adolescent, and should be taught with love, respect, and great care. The allowance should not break your own budget, either. You may just transfer whatever you have budgeted for your child on a weekly basis to him. He will learn to use the money wisely, under you supervision, if necessary. Your child should also learn to save up for "big ticket" items. After all, you have to do the same. It is life.

Empowerment

Parents should guide the adolescent child by empowering him to make decisions. Again, start with simple decisions like what clothes to wear or what hair styles to have. That will do no harm to anybody. At the same time, the adolescent learns from the feedback of peers whether he is making the right choice. With the techniques of natural and logical consequences, your youngster will soon learn how to make appropriate choices and decisions. You will find that he has to be responsible for himself no matter where or when. This is another powerful tool for parents. We all know that we cannot follow our youngster around all the time. The only person that follows him around all day is himself. He has to be accountable to himself. He cannot lie to himself.

Several rules apply here. First, we obey the laws of our society. The laws are made for the common good. It is not the parent's law. It is society's law that we all obey and abide by. Should he break the law, he is responsible for it. Explain the laws simply to children, making them aware that it is the same laws that you abide and follow, and you will not shield them from any law enforcement activities. Simply, they are responsible for what they do. Parents love them, but will not bail them out of jail should jail-time be necessary. You can go to the jail and visit him because you still love him. And, since he is smart enough to get himself there, he is responsible for serving the time and getting himself out of there. Secondly, do not be critical about the decision he made. After all, it was his decision. Do not offer suggestions unless you are asked for your opinion because you do not want to be blamed for the awkward outcome of the decision. Again, let natural and logical consequences work the wonders. Your child will learn. Thirdly, encourage the youngster to make plans for himself. It can be a short-term plan, an intermediate-term plan, or a long-term plan. This will teach your youngster to focus on what he really wants to do. Plans can be modified later after consciously thinking about them over time. This technique trains the youngster to think and analyze what he wants to do and achieve in a certain mount of time. Teach the youngster to set goals, goals that are reachable with some effort, and not dreams that have no reality. This will create hope, a sense of accomplishment, and build self-image. A big project can be broken down into small pieces, and attempts made to conquer a small piece at a time. In this way, the youngster can observe and learn the needed problem-solving skills which will be beneficial for him for a lifetime. Empowering the youngster to be his own guardian has many other advantages. This will decrease the conflicts you may experience with your adolescent children. After all, you are empowering him to be responsible for himself. You are there to guide him, but not to guard him. He is his own guardian. With this concept, you are free. With the caring and nurturing that you have done in the previous years, you will find that time and again your youngster will shine in making decisions, and you will be proud of him.

Dating/Courtship

During the early adolescent years, friends are important to the youngster. Most early adolescent children hang around with members of the same sex; however, there are situations when opposite sex friends will invite your child to parties or gatherings. It is absolutely all right for them to go. Again, you need to trust your youngster's judgment. In particular, when boys and girls grow up together, they will treat each other like brothers and sisters and will not deliberately hurt each other. This will give them the experience to make decisions in front of the opposite sex without feeling embarrassed, shy, or timid. The earlier they master the skill of meeting opposite sex friends, the better they will feel about the situation and make rational decisions without the fear of how to handle the first date. Here, respect and fun can be accomplished and both boys and girls can learn to like each other's company. The relationship can mature to a meaningful one, or at the very least, both parties will learn from the experience. Parents do not need to arrange for this courtship, but parents should not be in the way either. This kind of relationship should be developed naturally.

Chemical Dependency Prevention

At this age of early adolescence, youngsters are constantly exposed to the chemical dependent world; this includes drugs of abuse, tobacco smoking and chewing, and alcohol ranging from mouthwash to hard liquor. All of these items are easily available to the early adolescent youngster. Literally speaking, one cannot avoid the exposure of the youngster to these substances. "Just say no" is a slogan; however, it depends on the deeper meaning of the slogan to influence the youngster. The youngster needs to have a very good self-image, knowing that he will face different temptations all the time to use these substances. Here, the law also applies. Maybe it is all right for adults to smoke cigarettes, chew tobacco, or drink alcoholic beverages, but it is against the law for the minor person to do the same. It may be difficult to explain to the youngster the reasoning behind this; however, it is not difficult to explain the responsibility of one's action involving the substance. Empowerment is also very important here, knowing that one has to trust the youngster since he is the only person who can follow himself all the time. Develop a dialogue about chemical dependency with the adolescent child. Let him know that the temptation and peer pressure are there. It is totally up to him to try the first cigarette, the first drink, or the first "joint". He will be his own judge to see if the "high" is worth the risk of being caught. Other than the risk taking behavior, self development is also crucial in the determination of drug dependency. Parents can develop challenges for youngsters, involving them in extra-curricular activities and developing the "natural high" that we all possess in our own body. It has been observed that the chemical use behavior normally starts as experimentation during early adolescent years, and subsequently evolves into an escape phenomenon, using chemicals to bury oneself and escape reality. By helping the youngster discover his own self and develop a good self-image, you can help him to resist the temptation of a "quick-fix" type of mentality and to delay his gratification.

Planning

Early adolescent children should be encouraged to make plans for their future. When entering middle school, the youngster will be able to see how he positions himself in the family, in school, and in society as he matures. Forming a concrete plan of action gives the youngster a lot of freedom to explore the future, finding out what he likes, how he achieves the plan, and most of all, finding and recognizing himself and his role in the family and in society. Write down the plans. Turning plans into actions and creating goals and steps for him to follow is a lot of fun and a meaningful exercise to perform so that he can measure the outcome and success by looking back on his achievement. Parents can help him by exploring with the youngster, guiding him, teaching him different ways to achieve what he wants, and turning his plans into reality. By making such a plan every six-weeks or so, he can chart his progress, particularly in school work, getting along with peers, and participation in family activities. This will also give an opportunity for the parents to interact with the youngster in a positive way to guide him through the difficult adolescent years. It is advisable for the youngster to learn to write a journal on a daily basis and to plan for the next day. This helps the youngster stay focused on his goals and learn to self-motivate. Through the daily entry, he learns to use his time wisely and efficiently, and he may accomplish a lot more if he can organize his time in such a way that no efforts are duplicated or wasted. This is an important habit that needs to be formed no later than early adolescence.

Safety Issues

Accident prevention programs are important for the early adolescent years. Youngsters learn to assume risk-taking behaviors in sports, at home, and at school. Four-wheelers, skateboards, and roller-blades can all be dangerous to the youngster without proper supervision and protective gear when engaging in these activities. Similarly, power-tools, lawn equipment, and exercise equipment around the house all need good role modeling and teaching on proper usage, storage, and cleaning. Youngsters have to learn to respect these useful tools and use them properly and safely, and then they will have many years of enjoyment, recreation, and work. Accidents claim most of the lives during the adolescent years. This is the number one killer as well as the number one disabler. Do not let your love ones fall victim to the mostly preventable misadventures in life.

The discussion on the above topics can be done with the adolescent present with the parents. If there are objections or differences in opinion, the youngster should be allowed to speak in a civil manner. Eventually, the parents still make the final decision the youngster will abide by most of the time. If you have other questions and queries, you may make another appointment for a conference or other counseling session.

Immunization records should be reviewed before the conclusion of the office visit. If the adolescent did not receive the hepatitis B vaccine during infancy, the parents should be encouraged to have the youngster vaccinated against hepatitis B because of the possible development of the chronic carrier state and the future development of hepatocellular carcinoma of the liver. If the youngster did not receive the second dose of the measles, mumps and rubella vaccine, this is also a good time to give it. Hepatitis A vaccine should be given if the youngster did not receive it at an earlier age. A tuberculin skin test is strongly suggested during the early adolescent years because of the possible reactivation of tuberculosis at the onset of puberty. Tetanus and diphtheria vaccines are given once every five to ten years, and a booster shot may be necessary.

The Mid-Adolescent Years

By mid-adolescence, most youngsters are well into their pubertal development. Some girls may have already started their menstrual period, and most boys have also entered puberty. They notice a lot of changes in their body. They may have a lot of questions about themselves and be unwilling or uncomfortable asking their parents. They may find it difficult to find answers by themselvers or by talking with their friends. They frequently turn to their physician for answers, particularly if they have developed a good rapport with their pediatrician. Most pediatricians feel comfortable discussing many of these issues with their adolescent patients.

Commonly, it is the school/sports physical that leads the adolescent into the physician's office for a routine examination. It is imperative for the youngster to understand that this examination will take time, so please schedule it well ahead of time and let the physician's office know so that the staff can set aside enough time for this particular visit. This visit may coincide with the entrance into high school. The youngster will need guidance from professionals who have experience working with and understanding the mentality of the adolescent.

Ideally speaking, you should have a rough agenda forwarded to the physician's office to prepare the office for the different topics and questions you may have. Similarly, your physician may give you a list of topics that may be discussed during the visit. This is beneficial for both parties so that you will not feel that the time you spent in the office is a waste, and you get the most out of the visit. It is common for the parents not to accompany the youngster to these visits; however, one would strongly urge at least one of the parents to attend. This will make the youngster feel that this kind of periodic check-up is important, both to him as well as the family.

By mid-adolescent years, the youngster feels that his peer group is extremely important. Parents should be sensitive to this aspect of development. You may or may not approve of all the things that are going on in his circle. However, one should always separate the behavior that one observes from the person. You may not like the behavior of your son, yet you need to accept him as your equal and not downgrade him. It is particularly important for parents to realize that none of us are perfect, either. Be friends with your son, yet be analytical of his behavior. You can point out your observations and have a discussion with your adolescent, yet refrain from remarking that you dislike his friends. All of us have our strengths and weaknesses. We can all learn from our faults and promote our strengths to beautify our society. At this age when their moral developmental stage reaches maturity (stage six of Kolberg's moral development), the adolescent may easily see that we, parents and members of the adult world, are ambivalent on a lot of issues and are bigots on certain sets of values. This makes life very difficult for the adolescent. With their idealism of how the world should be and how the world is, they see a constant conflict with themselves, their parents, and their authoritative figures. Role-modeling is extremely important for this age group, be it at home, at school, or with their peer group. Accept the challenge from your teenagers. Discuss issues with them. Try to separate the issues of argument from the teenager, always reminding him that you will be there for him whatever his decision may be.

Mid-Adolescent Girls

By mid-adolescence, most girls have already started their menstrual periods. They may view it as an inconvenience or a nuisance, but they need to learn to accept it with grace and manage it on a monthly basis so as not to let it interfere with their lifestyle. After all, they are going to have many more years of menstrual periods before menopause occurs. Teach them how to control the cramps with non-steroidal, anti-inflammatory agents like ibuprofen, and how to be careful with personal hygiene during their period. Teach them to avoid tampons, particularly the ultra-absorbent ones, since they are linked to the development of toxic-shock syndrome, a highly fatal disease that can be easily prevented. Mid-cycle abdominal pain is also very common at this age since most of them are ovulating on a regular basis. Let them learn to take charge of these events. However, if dysmenorrhoea or mittelschmerz are incapacitating to the youngster, proper gynecological evaluation should be obtained and managed accordingly.

The youngster should be guided to the examination room with proper instructions on undressing and changing into an examination gown. Height and weight are recorded and plotted on the growth curve as usual. Skin-fold thickness is optional for the teenager, whereas blood pressure, visual screen and hearing screen should be done routinely. Specific concerns and complaints from the teenager are recorded by the nursing staff and prepared for the physician. If the young girl is apprehensive about the visit, a female staff member may accompany the youngster during the examination, particularly if she comes without her parents.

After greeting the youngster, but before the examination, the physician should make sure that the youngster is comfortable. Chatting with the young lady, addressing her concerns and complaints may make the visit a little more pleasant and relieve any anxiety she may have about the visit. Weight, skin care, and nutrition are common concerns and should be addressed systematically. Personal hygiene should be emphasized, particularly regular cleansing of her skin, which may cut down the severity of the development of cystic acne. Sun-tanning instructions should be provided specifically, since solar injury to the skin may leave permanent damage in future years. This is particularly important in early spring when the young lady is preparing for summer exposure on beaches and at swimming pools. A balanced diet with all the appropriate food groups in the right proportions will eliminate unhealthy dieting and the up and down swing of body weight. Appropriate dietary supplements are also important as a menstruating young lady will need extra iron and calcium to account for the monthly losses. Physical activities should also be encouraged. One can always point out that if one is planning to enjoy a feast, one just needs to work off the excess calories to maintain balance.

A physical examination will follow in the usual manner, with particular reference to the skin, acne development, and the other systems associated with puberty. As indicated in early adolescence, puberty thyroid enlargement is common, and one needs to assess the functional aspect of the thyroid gland. Be it hyperthyroidism or hypothyroidism, the appropriate diagnosis is important for the proper management. The spine should be checked; however, it should not be a threat any more. With the start of menarche, spine growth will slow down and stop within the next two years. A sudden, significant collapse of the spine into scoliosis is not likely to happen. Auscultation to the heart should be done both in lying and sitting positions. This will facilitate the detection of mitral valve prolapse, which may occur in about five percent of all adolescent girls. This is significant since they need to be protected from subacute bacterial endocarditis before dental work as well as sudden arrhythmias during exercise and stress.

Exercise tolerance, joint mobility, muscle strength, and deep tendon reflexes are assessed in the normal manner. Tanner staging of sexual development should be performed and recorded with particular reference to breast development. A staff member should demonstrate self-examination of the breast, either by a model or through a pre-recorded video. It should be stressed to the teenager that she needs to do it on a monthly basis particularly after the menstrual flow. She should report to her parents or be assessed by the physician if there is irregularity, nodularity, and tenderness present in her breasts. If the youngster is sexually active, appropriate advice on contraception and prevention of sexually transmitted diseases should be discussed, and a pelvic examination, including a Pap-smear, should be done on an annual basis.

Mid-Adolescent Boys

By about fourteen years of age, most boys are either at the beginning of mid-adolescence or finishing up early adolescence. The entrance into the high school years heralds the final countdown of the compulsory school years and the insecurity of venturing into maturity. Emotionally, most teenage boys yearn for acceptance by their peers and being recognized by them is an important aspect of their achievement. The rebellious ideas, the fights with their parents, the risk-taking behaviors are all part of this stage of development. This is also the time when they start to experience their own hormonal surge, even though this is not as marked as the girls' "premenstrual syndrome," the so-called "pre-man syndrome" does exist. They have similar rage, tantrums, and periods of inconsolable moodiness, just like adolescent girls. Acceptance is important here, knowing that engaging them in fights, both verbally and physically, will deliver a bruised ego to both parties that may take a long time to heal. This does not mean that you have to yield. Judicial use of logical and natural consequences, and reflecting their behavior back to them will serve as useful management tools for parents. It is particularly important for mothers to learn to use these techniques as they may see that physical and corporal punishment will not work and may have severe repercussions. Provide choices instead of commands, make requests when you need help, and offer suggestions when you are asked. Give your younger the liberty to choose so that he can learn to make decisions and be responsible for them. Guide him instead of guarding him. After all, your job is to nurture him to successful adulthood.

As the office staff guides the youngster into the examination room, he will be instructed to take off all his clothes except the underwear (with or without a gown) and wait for the nurse to perform all the measurements. Weight, height, blood pressure, and vital signs are taken, recorded, and plotted against the standard curves. Optional hearing and visual screens are done, with particular reference to color-blindness which is inherited in a sex-link recessive manner and up to five percent of boys may be affected. The physical examination will proceed as usual. Particularly for tall boys, examination of the spine is important now since they are entering the rapid height growth stage of their development. The incidence of scoliosis in boys is less than in girls; however, it does exist to a certain degree, and this is the time to find it. Again, early detection may provide a chance for remedial exercise, postural training, and physical therapy. Acne may be a common nuisance. The teenager should be taught basic skin hygiene to avoid scarring and further re-infection of the lesions. The cardiovascular system is examined in the usual manner with particular reference to blood pressure. Both sitting and recumbent blood pressure should be obtained. This should be compared with the normal range for the particular age group. If necessary, appropriate counseling will be provided with regards to diet, salt intake, exercise habit, and cigarette smoking. Joint mobility, exercise tolerance, muscle strength, and deep tendon reflexes are assessed and recorded. Assessment of the Tanner staging of sexual development should be done. The teaching of self-examination of the testicles is important for mid-adolescent boys. Using a model, teach him to feel for abnormal lumps and sparing the normal epididymis may accomplish this goal. Just like the breast self-examination in girls, this should be done on a monthly basis. It can easily be accomplished during a shower without the restriction of the girls needing to wait until after the menstrual period.

Most of the topics for discussion on early adolescence apply here also, with special remarks on how he is getting along with his family. The following topics are chosen for further discussion, specifically because of the age group and their maturity.

Sexuality

With raging hormones, most adolescent youngsters have experienced sexual drive, particularly in our current permissive society. Temptations abound, ranging from the printed press to television shows and movies that give the idea of the permissibility of pre-marital sexual encounters. However, the willingness to participate in any such act depends upon the adolescent and his self-development and self esteem. Other than rape or incest, the adolescent participates willingly with the full understanding of the consequences.

Their participation may be because of curiosity, risk-taking behavior, forbidden-fruit syndrome, or even to sustain a desired effect, namely, to draw the attention of the adult members of the family who may be a distant biological father or the mother who is too involved in her work or herself. Parents should be able to lay down the guiding principles for the teenagers. The teenagers should be held accountable for their own actions since no parent can follow their teenagers 24 hours a day, every day of the year. Teenagers should be taught the risk of premarital sex, from untimely pregnancy to the development of sexually transmitted diseases. They should be taught the right to honor celibacy and the joy of fulfillment on their wedding day without the fear of their own conscience and burden that may eventually take a toll on their marriages.

Masturbation amongst teenagers is common, if not universal. It has never been shown that occasional masturbation hurts anybody, and parents may well be advised to leave the teenagers alone on this issue. "Wet dreams" for teenage boys are normal and common. They do not even indicate a conscious masturbation. It may just be the normal nocturnal ejaculation, a physiological phenomenon that signals sexual maturity.

Homosexuality is currently held as another biological state that parents do not have a major influence on, and they certainly do not need to feel guilty for it. Parents are encouraged to welcome the teenager's friends, accept them, teach them and guide them, posting the big picture in front of the teenager instead of bickering about issues that they do not have any control over, forcing the teenagers to react out of anger or lack of self-control into deeper troubles than their initial intent. Support their decisions, be it celibacy or otherwise, for they need to learn the consequence of their decisions and how to prevent and protect themselves from the unwanted effects, enjoying a healthy sex life in the years to come as mature adults.

Responsibility

Responsibility is a developmental task. No one is born responsible. We develop a sense of responsibility through a long process of learning, trial and error, and, most of all, through the practice of being responsible. One cannot demand responsibility just because one reaches a certain age or a certain level of maturity. On the other hand, if one is given a certain task to perform with a sense of expectation, one learns to be responsible. This starts at a very young age by helping around the house, through the experience of natural consequences, and later on, logical consequences. One learns to act rather than react. Through the early years in primary grades, one learns to be responsible for one's own product in school work and school performance. Thus, it is important for parents to learn that it is the youngster's responsibility to do homework, to remember to bring it to school, and to hand it in on time to the appropriate teachers. It is not the parent's job to do that. The parents have already had their turn when they were at school. The teachers should learn to hold the youngster accountable and be responsible for his assignment, rather than drawing the innocent parents into this battlefield. Similarly, the responsibility of keeping one's own property, room, hygiene and appearance are all being developed as the youngster grows and matures. We cannot hold a two-year-old child responsible for any task because the two-year-old child has not learned to be responsible. At the same time, if a sixteen year old adolescent has never been held responsible for anything, he will not be responsible for anything. Naturally, as one emerges from the "amoral stage" of moral development from birth to about eighteen months of age, one needs to learn to be responsible for oneself for simple events. Gradually, as one matures throughout the different stages of development, one learns to be responsible for more complex tasks, including self-motivation, self-discipline, self-awareness and self-policing of one's own actions regardless of whether one is being watched or not. This sense of responsibility is very important for the adolescent youngster because soon he will be held accountable for all of his actions. Please remember, responsibility is being developed. One cannot demand responsibility just because of one's age. Offer opportunities to your youngster to develop his responsibility early. Under your guidance, let you child learn to be responsible for all his daily activities, like eating, drinking, going to the bathroom, etc. at an early age. Utilize natural and logical consequences to teach responsibility. Through your role modeling and guidance, your youngster will learn to be responsible. At the same time, you also need to demonstrate trust and respect for your youngster's decisions in order to booster your child's self-confidence and self-esteem.

Motivation

Motivation is also a learned phenomenon. One cannot demand motivation. As the youngster sees things completed or not depending on his actions, he will learn to set priorities and achieve what he thinks is optimal for his situation. If he does not see the necessity to perform, he will not perform. This consequence should be his problem. One can teach motivation by learning to set goals and limits. Knowing one's limit and knowing that one only has twenty four hours in a day, one will need some time for rest, meals, and personal hygiene, so one should set goals that are achievable with certain amount of effort. One would feel encouraged and motivated having a sense of accomplishment. On the contrary, if the goals are set too high and not achievable despite a reasonable effort, one may feel defeated, discouraged, and a sense of despair. Self-motivation is such an important task in the development of the self that one needs to let youngsters learn this skill early in their lifetime. By learning to set realistic goals and accomplishments, one learns to self-motivate. It is too often that we see parents shouting orders to youngsters, rather than letting the youngsters learn to self-motivate. This is actually a waste of the parents' energy and is detrimental to the youngster's self-development. Through the experience of natural consequences, the youngster should learn in the formative years that self-motivation is important and the rewards are plenty. Parents should be there to facilitate this process rather than hinder the development by giving too many commands that build resentment particularly during the middle adolescent years.

Planning

Upon entering high school, the mid-adolescent youngster should have a clear understanding of his future career and what he wants to accomplish in the next four years of schooling. Parents should be there to guide and assist in the career planning and goal setting. For the college bound student, parents may want to sit down with the teenager and work out a schedule with him to provide a solid plan for the future. For an average family, it is prudent to plan ahead so that finances will not be a hindrance for the student. Look into available funds, loans, and scholarships for various vocations and careers. If you plan ahead, the chance for you to achieve your goal is just so much better.

A bright student should stay focused on the goals he sets and ignore the financial burden. It is still true that if you get a perfect or near perfect score (between fifteen hundred and sixteen hundred points) on your Scholastic Achievement Test (S.A.T.) almost all universities in the United States will provide you with scholarships and enough for room, board, and tuition plus some spending money. Just do a little calculation with your youngster: ten extra mathematical problems a day in four years time means an extra ten thousand problems. An extra ten new words in the vocabulary everyday would mean ten thousand new words. These practices will do wonders on the results of the standardized tests as measured by the S.A.T.

Most youngsters have in their mind that they want to work outside the home for spending money in their spare time, maybe twenty hours a week, at the most. However, by simple calculation, one can demonstrate to the youngsters that working for minimum wage for two years will not pay as handsomely as a four-year scholarship to an Ivy League school. Yes, one has to realize that the deferment of gratification for any individual is difficult. However, it is through this self-discipline that great individuals are trained. As for the non-college bound, one can still guide them to the vocation they choose, working towards the goals that they want for themselves so that they will not be regretful for the rest of their lives.

Moreover, learning is a life-long process. One can always learn. Taking classes at local colleges or simply learning on the job can be very fulfilling. Parents should not have preconceived ideas of what their child's future career should be. Any vocation can be successful and fulfilling. Mother Teresa of Calcutta never thought that serving the poorest of the poor and sickest of the sick would win her a Nobel Prize. Parents are there to guide the youngster at this stage - you cannot force or manipulate your mid-adolescent any more. They are individuals with feelings, determination, and visions of their own future.

Allowance

By mid-adolescence, most teenagers would like to have some pocket money to spend, whether it is for going to the movies with friends or buying little things for birthdays or holidays. It is appropriate for the parents to provide an adequate amount for the teenager for supplies and spending money with no strings attached. As indicated in the early adolescent years, one can add to the responsibility of what the spending money is for. Instead of just lunch money, one can add supply money, gas money, and trip money so that the youngster will learn how to budget for the rest of his or her life. Even though the United States of America is the richest country in the world, without proper budget training for our senators, they manage to have deficit spending, creating a national debt of more than seven trillion dollars, without feeling guilty or shameful about their accomplishment. No one single person can afford to live without a budget. Everyone needs to develop a sense of fiscal responsibility by learning to handle money wisely, to bargain, and to save for rainy days.

By mid-adolescence, one should have the basic skills of accounting and budgeting, otherwise, he can run into deep trouble by the time he or she is college-bound. The allowance can be increased gradually from lunch money to all the necessities for the whole semester. Again, an allowance should be provided for the teenager. He does not need to "earn" it. It is given as a token of love and that needs to be emphasized. "Mother and father know that you need to spend some money, and we love you and care for you, therefore we provide for you," is an important message that all adolescent youngsters need to hear. Soon, they will realize how important this unconditional love and respect is to them, and it also plants a seed for them to care for your old age.

Respect

There is an old Chinese saying: "Even dogs and horses are being fed; if there is no respect (to the old or the young), what is the difference?"

Respect is mutual. If you treat your teenage youngster just like you treat your servant or your maid, they will feel like your servant or your maid and will not take an extra step to work and beautify your home environment. It is true that the habits of self-motivation and self-respect need to be developed early during the formative years by the methods of natural and logical consequences (see previous chapters). After all, parents surely would not like to be treated as servants or maids in their old age by their children to earn support from them.

Learn to respect your adolescent children. Respect their friends and their decisions. Let them be responsible for their decisions and handle the consequences of their decisions. They will learn. They will improve their decision making skills. They should earn your respect by producing results of their work - their athletic performances, their school work, their self-discipline, their self motivation, and their own planning.

Courage

It is important for the mid-adolescent youngster to develop a sense of courage - the courage of self-acceptance, knowing that he may not be as perfect as his parents' desire. This is a vital issue for the adolescent to learn before moving on to adulthood. None of us are perfect. A star football player at school may not be the top student; a straight A student may not be able to sing or dance. All of us have some kind of "learning disability;" learning to accept oneself is as important as learning to walk or learning to eat. After all, one can learn from one's mistakes and shortcomings to overcome difficulties and move on. With this attitude, the youngster may develop courage to pursue any task or try any difficult assignment without the fear of failure. The courage to accept imperfection is important to resolve when the youngster enters high school, where the subjects are getting more complex and difficult to master, the teachers are more demanding, and the peer pressure is ever rising. One needs to have the courage to set one's own goals and pursue them, accept the imperfection, and get on with one's life.

Chemical Dependency

This topic is high on most parents' agenda; however, the teenage youngster is very much aware of it, particularly in today's high schools. The most common chemicals used are still alcohol, cigarettes, and possibly marijuana. These are in every high school and may even be in every middle school. It is not a matter of exposure to them, but rather a matter of one's control over the effect of these chemicals. Role modeling is very important. One cannot point a finger at a teenager's joint while wearing a cigarette on one's lip. Action speaks louder than words. At the same time, a teenager can always be deceitful to parents, teachers, and law-enforcement officials alike. However, a teenager cannot cheat himself! He has to be answerable to himself.

Chemical dependency is an "escape phenomenon," meaning that other than just curiosity, one wants to utilize chemicals to blunt one's pain of real life events and escape reality. Involving teenagers in different activities that are meaningful to them will curtail the utilization of chemicals for escape from reality or to boost one's image. With good role-modeling at school and at home, with friends and peers, your child will like other self-gratifying activities without needing to venture into drug usage. Self-development is the most important deterrent to habitual chemical usage in our teenage children. Trusting them, giving them responsibility, and letting them self-govern are some of the key points in dealing with the issue of drug abuse and chemical dependency.

There are many other important topics one can discuss during a mid-adolescent periodic physical examination session. With the above topics, one hopes to cover the more commonly asked questions and topics.

Before the physician leaves the examination, he or she will review the immunization status. Diphtheria and tetanus toxoid should be given at least once every five to ten years. If the teenager has not received the hepatitis B vaccine or the hepatitis A vaccine, he or she should be urged to receive this series of shots, also.

The Late Adolescent Years

When young people call the doctor's office for an appointment, they have something on their mind. Now in late adolescence, it is rather uncommon for parents to accompany them to the office. Usually, he has a minor aliment or some burning issue and needs someone to discuss it with. Or, perhaps it is about a college entrance physical examination. (Some colleges may still require it, but mostly they just ask for a verification of vaccination status.) It can also be a pre-employment physical examination. While the youngster may want to talk to the doctor for known exposure to drugs, alcohol, or some diseases, they may or may not want the prospective employer to know. These are just a few reasons for the late adolescent youngster to come to the doctor. There may be other reasons as well. Routine physical examinations are still encouraged by the American Academy of Pediatrics. This is also the normal "exit physical" for the pediatrician who may not be following the youngster any longer, transferring the care to either a family physician or a general internist for subsequent health maintenance encounters in the years to come. It should also be a joyous occasion for the pediatrician since he or she has successfully guided, monitored, and advised the parents from the pre-conceptional idea of venturing into parenthood through infancy to maturity, from innocence to righteousness, through the formative years to a mature citizen in the society, bearing productive fruit of matrimony to a succession of the next generation.

By this time, most late adolescent youngsters know their position is in the family, school, around their peers, and in society. The late adolescent reaches full maturity, settling down from the idealistic mid-adolescent years, not being as argumentative as he was, and being much more realistic about what the future may bring and promise. He is at the post-conventional stage of moral development, able to see the other person's perspective and reasoning, and make judgments and decisions according to his own experience and education. He may come to the doctor's office with some anxiety, a form of separation anxiety, knowing that his days at home are limited and that soon he will be on his own. This separation anxiety presents the other side of a late adolescent. He may be lonely and fearful of the unknown, be it college or a new job, uncertain about himself, and unsure about his ability to survive and thrive in the real world. The pediatrician is in a very good position to counsel the youngster, since he or she may have been caring for the youngster all his life. The pediatrician is able to act as a friend, an authority, and a trusted individual that the youngster may have confidence in and be able to communicate with. More importantly, the doctor may also be able to talk to the parents as an advocate for the young adult to bridge the gap that may have developed during the argumentative years of mid-adolescence. This may also be an opportunity for the pediatrician to point out the strengths and weaknesses of the young adult without being incriminating or judgmental, to direct him forward with a concrete plan for the future years to serve society.

As the young adult enters the waiting area, he may feel a little awkward being surrounded by babies and toddlers, reflecting upon his own younger years. Hopefully, the receptionist will greet this person fairly soon in the examination area where the patient will be instructed to undress and change into the examination gown to be weighed and measured. Vital signs, including supine and sitting blood pressure measurements are taken and the patient waits for the physician to come for the physical examination and some anticipatory guidance as he or she normally would do. Optional screens may include hearing screen, vision screen, body composition analysis or skin fold thickness, exercise tolerance, peak flow screening as indicated by history, examination, and requirements to fulfill the accompanying forms or inquiry that the youngster may bring to the examination. The youngster should also be advised to bring in a list of questions that he may want to ask the doctor in advance so that the doctor may have time to prepare for them.

When the doctor enters the examination room, he or she will greet the youngster with a broad smile, shaking hands, and finally settling down for the information gathering part of the examination.

Nutritional history is an important aspect of this encounter. The young person may have various questions about this topic as well. In our modern American society, we are very health conscious. However, imbalanced diets and misinformation about nutrition are common. Some youngsters are too busy to sit down and eat, some are anorexic because of concerns about weight gain, some may overeat because of anxiety, and some may be under-nourished because of misconceptions about a balanced diet. By plotting the growth curve, height/weight ratio, and skin fold thickness of the youngster, the physician can gently point out that over-eating leads to obesity as does eating the wrong groups of food for the wrong reasons, and point out the advantage of a balanced diet on one's daily activity. All these are important for the late adolescent to hear and learn, since he will soon be making these decisions independently without aid from parents. Calcium supplementation is important for the adolescent as well.

It is really okay to drink water on a routine basis instead of milk or soft drinks. After all, even diet soft drinks provide extra calories and may contain stimulants that one may want to avoid. The four basic food groups should be outlined in such a manner that the adolescent may easily follow them. Small, frequent meals instead of binge eating at the end of the day is usually good advice for the college bound, and a regular, three meals a day schedule will suit most working individuals. They need to learn to be flexible with their own schedule and able to modify it as they see fit, learning the basic principles of good nutrition. This may enhance good health, prevent sickness, and improve endurance at work, in school, and help them maintain their youthful figure for a much longer period of time.

Further history will reveal the nature of the examination, be it a pre-employment physical or for a specific purpose, and the physician will address the various issues as they present themselves. Adolescents will have the idea of infallibility and the myth that they are resistant to all ills. A word of caution from their trusted physician may be of benefit to them for a long time. Topics like risk-taking behaviors, personal hygiene, self-control, acknowledgment of other persons' rights, respect for others, and acceptance of one's challenges are appropriate topics for advice and warrant a brief discussion. Sex education, prevention of unwanted pregnancies, and prevention of sexually transmitted diseases are important for the maturing adolescent, with their raging sex hormones, to help them bear in mind that in the heat of passion, accidents may happen that they may regret for the rest of their lives. So they need to learn to be prepared and be cool about any situation they may encounter. Self-motivation, self-recognition, and self-discipline are the keys to success in society, and they need to learn to master their opportunities as they appear in their lifetime. The concept of responsibility to oneself, to one's family, and to society needs to be stressed emphatically to the youngster.

A brief but thorough physical examination will be performed systematically with emphasis on areas of concern.

Late Adolescent Girls

In addition to the above information gathering, a detailed history of the menstrual cycle should be obtained with the character of the flow, the length of the period, the amount of estimated blood loss (numbers of pads or tampons used in a day), the quality of the cramps, and the effects on school performance are recorded on the chart. This may form a basis for further discussion with the young lady about appropriate gynecological referral and evaluation.

By late adolescence, most girls know how to take care of their skin, how to use skin cleansers, and apply make-up appropriately. They seldom need further advice from their doctors. However, in problem cases with cystic acne or psoriasis, dermatological consultation may be necessary.

Heart and cardiovascular systems are evaluated in the normal manner with particular reference to mitral valve prolapse which is common in girls.

Thyroid function status should also be evaluated because both hyperthyroidism and thyroiditis are common in teenage adolescent girls. Palpation of the abdomen, including abdominal palpation of the pelvis, can be performed on a well-relaxed youngster. Pelvic examination may or may not be performed at the preference of the physician. For sexually active adolescent girls, a Pap smear with the appropriate vaginal cultures should be done on an annual basis. Examination of the breast, evaluation of the Tanner staging, and the technique of self-examination of the breast should be taught and demonstrated to the young lady, emphasizing to her that this examination needs to be done monthly after the end of her menstrual flow.

Late Adolescent Boys

By the time they graduate from high school, some adolescent boys may just be entering the late adolescent stage of their development. They may still have more physical growth over the next few years. It is not uncommon to find that upon entering college some boys may grow four or five more inches in their freshman year. Examination of the spine remains an important evaluation during this visit. Unfortunately, there is no effective way for the youngster to learn to self-examine the spine. However, this needs to be mentioned to him specifically so that he may seek advice and evaluation by a health care professional on a regular basis, maybe once every six months or so, if the peak growth velocity has not passed during this "exit" examination.

Late adolescent boys may be very hairy, with facial hair and body hair growing everywhere. Personal hygiene is important for him to understand. He is the only person who can care for him all the time now. Advice on skin care can be provided, with the appropriate consultation to dermatologists for resistant acne and persistent fungal infection of the groin, feet, etc.

Muscle strength and joint mobility are important evaluations, particularly if the youngster is going to be involved in sports in college. Examination of the cardiovascular systems may include exercise tolerance. Pulmonary functions, chest excursions, peak-flow, and vital capacities are also important in the evaluation for athletic performance. Palpation of the abdomen with particular reference to the hernial orifices is important, especially for the weight lifting and muscle building exercises. Examination of the external genitalia, determination of the Tanner staging, and the teaching of the self-examination technique for the testicles are done in a systemic manner. It should be emphasized to the adolescent that most cancers of the testis occur between the ages of fifteen and twenty-five and that the adolescent is the one who discovers it most of the time. This examination needs to be done on a monthly basis, typically after a hot shower. Models are available for the youngster to learn to perform this important examination.

Other than the topics outlined in the previous paragraph, important discussions may include:

Interpersonal Interaction Skills

This is an important skill for the late adolescent to master. He is held accountable for all individual decisions and actions. His actions, reactions, and skills in dealing with friends, colleagues, and teachers will determine his future success. It is important for him to learn that there is no absolute right or wrong any more in most cases. He needs to determine the different shades of grey instead of black or white as it used to be at home or in school. He needs to stand on the principles that he believes in and is proud of. He is now an important individual in society and needs to have personal integrity so as not to be manipulated by others opinions, yet he needs to be sensitive to others. It is impossible to live in one's own little world. Interpersonal interaction makes one recognized by peers and helps one to be a well-adjusted individual in society. He needs to learn to respect other people - their ideas, opinions, and points of view. At the same time, he needs to earn respect from others. This is an important task wherever he may be. This skill needs to be pointed out to the youngster at this stage of development to pave a successful road for his future and his career in life.

Budget

By now, most late adolescent youngsters should have a fair idea of how to budget on a continual basis, be it the allowance that the parents give them or their own money earned by working at different jobs outside the home. They should be encouraged to have a checking account and maybe a credit card. Yes, these are temptations for youngsters, but through the temptations they learn to be responsible. They also learn that by saving money before they spend it, they will have more money to spend. Otherwise, the bank and the credit card company will all share part of his income in the form of interest. By the time they are seniors in high school, they can figure out the basic reasons for the banks or credit card companies lending them money. It is always a good idea to encourage them to save about ten percent of their income/allowance for unexpected expenses or holidays.

As they enter college, they need more discipline to budget even though they may have a scholarship or some form of a financial aid. As they move away from home without the readily available guidance from parents, they may have an urge to spend every penny they have for things that may not be essential for their survival in college. Also, they may not be able to run home to ask for money as easily as before. Those who plan to start work need to learn to live within their means and to balance their budget on a monthly basis. Those who may still be staying at home need to make a positive effort to pay their parents for rent, utilities, and food so that they can prepare for their own homes when they decide to move out of their parents' house. A lot of the late adolescent youngsters forget the fact that they receive subsidies from their parents for room and board and think they can spend liberally. As soon as they move out, they immediately feel the pinch when the subsidy from the parents is gone. They may encounter hardship. Good budgeting will solve these kinds of problems. They also need to learn to provide for their parents even if their parents do not depend on them. It is a way to say "thank you" for all the years of nurturing, support, and love. And parents should accept their gifts with grace. If the parents do not need to spend the money, it is a good idea to save it for the youngster or for gifts in later days. You will always find good uses for it later on if you really do not need the money. This also shows the adolescent's appreciation of the effort, love, and caring for the many years that their parents provided. It is time for them to show a token of their respect to their parents. Parents should be proud of this token of love, the fruit of their many years of hardship in bringing up their youngster.

Sexuality (To the late adolescent)

Statistics are alarming. More than seventy-five percent of all late adolescent boys have experienced sexual intercourse and more than fifty percent of high school girls have had similar encounters. However, you do not need to be part of the statistics. It all depends on the formation of morality and righteousness. Abstinence is a choice and celibacy can be a form of pride for the adolescent youngster to pursue. Putting it in another way, about twenty-five percent of adolescent boys and fifty percent of adolescent girls are virgins. It is up to the individual's choice, determination, and resistance to temptation to say "no" to the situations that one may not enjoy or consider right. Rape and incest aside, the individual needs to cooperate and respond to have a meaningful sexual relationship. Unless you are under the influence of drugs and alcohol, you are always in control of your body. If your boyfriend or girlfriend cannot respect your ideas and values now, how can he or she respect you later on in life? You can be part of the statistics - it is up to you to choose. If you decide to have premarital sexual relationships, make certain that you protect yourself against unwanted, untimely pregnancies and sexually transmitted diseases. Just imagine. If you have sexual intercourse with your mate, who may have had several other mates that he or she routinely has sex with, and each of these mates has several partners, you may be involved in the end result of a cumulative transmission with over a hundred individuals. Should one of these individuals have a disease that he or she may not want to disclose, you may have inadvertently received a dose of the microorganism. It is extremely difficult, in the heat of passion, to flash out a condom for use. And, worst of all, the protective effect of a properly inspected, rightfully used condom is only ninety percent. You are still unprotected at least ten percent of the time. Abstinence is an excellent alternative, and even self-satisfying masturbation can be an acceptable means of releasing one's sexual pressure.

Best of all, try to calm yourself down before you get overly excited and out of control. After all, the pride of virginity until matrimony is a lifelong honor. The only practical way of safe sex is abstinence, self-fulfillment, and possibly celibacy.

Planning

For the late adolescent youngster, planning for the future is a very important task that he must learn to master. This should not be news. Starting at the early adolescent stage, he should be taught how to plan for himself. By the late adolescent stage, the youngster should be an expert in planning for himself - daily, weekly, monthly, per semester, and per academic year. Long term planning is extremely important for this stage of development. It is through this planning process that he puts goals in front of him, giving these goals appropriate thought and consideration, setting up objectives, and proceeding with implementation. College planning, career planning, family planning, financial planning, and ultimately retirement planning are all important concepts for the youngster to learn. Plans can be modified as the time comes and after due consideration. This refinement and modification make life fun and dynamic. Yet, without conscientious planning efforts, life drifts on without purpose, and one loses sight of the future and the meaning of life.

Finally, the doctor wishes the youngster good luck and invites him to call and inform the office on how he is in the years to come.

PART

IV

Anticipatory Guidance

Nowadays, what do parents want? In general, we want to have happy, healthy children that grow up to be well-adjusted and successful. No one wants to have a son or daughter sit in jail. No one wants a growing seven trillion dollar national debt. No one wants to be a welfare recipient or on the unemployment payroll. Why have these things happened to us in this society? It is up to us, the people who form this society, to reform it so that we can restore honesty, integrity, faith, love, and charity to our nation and to mankind.

In the newborn nursery, one cannot distinguish who will be the future president or who will be locked behind bars. Everyone is born alike and innocent. Yes, there will be a lot of familial influence, yet that is not simply because of genetics. An adopted infant from a broken home at birth can be raised to be a responsible person. Those born with silver spoons in their mouths can be the black sheep of their families. There are many examples of such things in our society. By the time the same group of infants grow to three years of age, we find diversified personalities. Some are timid and shy, hiding behind their parents when confronted with a stranger; others are bold and self-confident, standing in front of you or me conversing like little adults and feeling good about themselves. Some are unruly, rough, and hyperactive; others are gentle, serene, and calm. In three short years, what happened?

It has been shown by various clinical psychologists that the first three years of life compile the crucial elements in the formation of personalities which determines how one feels and thinks about oneself in their lifetime. It is up to the individual child to determine how he feels about himself under a given situation. In the same situation, one individual may feel scared and timid while another feels at ease and comfortable. It depends on the makeup of the self with its foundation formed during the first three years of life.

All parents would like to impart the qualities of self-confidence, self-esteem, self-respect, and a positive self-image upon their children. Yet, an average infant between the age of nine months and three years of age and in the midst of their personality formation will be assaulted and bombarded with at least twenty "no, no's" per day by their caretaker, usually a loved one. Imagine if someone shouts twenty "no's" at you and then asks you to feel confident and secure about your next step and feel good about yourself. Yes, we do this to the next generation. Yet, we feel righteous in doing so without a sense of wrongdoing because mostly, we shout our "no, no's" because we love our children. Let's examine the situation. When a nine-month-old baby boy pulls up on the couch and starts to climb and his mother shouts "no, no don't climb," what does his mother mean? She doesn't mean that he should never climb or that he should be forbidden to climb. Instead, she means "Junior, I am afraid you may fall and hurt yourself." Obviously, this is a message of love from the mother. Yet, when the infant receives a negative command, he wanders on until receiving another, "no, no!" If he could communicate, he would ask, "What should I do?" Unfortunately, this situation occurs before he acquires the communicative skill of speaking. He wanders on, losing his confidence, his self-respect, and his self-image.

Since our motive is good and we are concerned about the danger of our loved ones, we can easily see this as an opportunity to guide the youngster to do the right thing by showing him how to climb, so he learns the skill and avoids a negative command. By using the technique of positive guidance and positive reinforcement, one helps the infant develop self-confidence, self-esteem, positive self-image, and respect. By using positive behavior modification techniques, one can physically remove the infant from danger and put him in a safe place, giving the infant other attractions so that he is out of danger. We should not feel threatened if the child throws a temper tantrum because of our actions. The concept of right/wrong and good/bad does not develop until two and a half to three years of age; therefore, the infant is reacting to his own frustration rather than to our authority. It is an excellent opportunity to teach tolerance of frustration which is essential for all children to learn.

Between the ages of three and six, your child is starting to form the concepts of morals and ethics. Typically, your youngster starts asking many questions. Every time you turn around, there is a "why" or a "how come." This is the stage of formation of reasoning, sequencing of events, and consequences. This is also the background of good citizenship. Why do criminals rob a bank, get arrested by the police, locked in jail, paroled, and released; go out and rob another bank and return to the cycle's beginning? Or, why does the same person who was laid off from one job and rehabilitated, accept a new job and then gets laid off again? Why do we have four to five generations of families who are on the welfare payroll? Why is their complaint that the government does not provide enough for them or that it is the government's fault that they have to live in such an environment? Why?

It is believed that during the formation of morals and ethics, something went wrong. To the robbers, the money they rob is the same as the money they earn. Of course, to the normal citizen, this makes a big difference. Yet, for the Department of Corrections to reform these individuals, it takes deep psychotherapy to reconstruct their moral makeup instead of just building more jails to house them. At least currently, it is possible for society to provide jails. To the unemployed, it is because no one has shown them the value of work and the enjoyment and satisfaction of accomplishing a day's work. How often does a mother explain to a three-year-old the importance of her going to work instead of cursing or feeling bad about going to work at same time telling the three-year-old that he should feel good about helping her work by picking up toys or dusting the furniture? Imagine putting yourself in the position of the employer. If you had an employee who only looked forward to coffee breaks, lunch hours, five p.m., Monday morning hangovers, and "thank God it's Friday," would you be able to run a business profitably in a capitalistic world? You would either end up terminating that employee or closing your operation.

During this stage of development, a parent should be prepared to answer all these questions. All the "whys" and "how comes" are opportunities for you to help your youngster form his standards based on what you want for him. Instead of the traditional "just because," "hush," "wait a minute," or "mommy's busy," one should try to answer the questions to the best of your ability with solid reasoning and information. Even if it is inconvenient or impossible for you to explain, you should still attempt to do so by bringing the youngster to the appropriate source to obtain the right answers. Those moments are the moments when your youngster is most apt to learn and absorb. Teach him. Be patient. You may need to answer and answer again because his questions will be repetitious. This is the only way he will learn. Do not expect him to remember just because you explained it to him once several weeks, days, or even minutes ago. After all, he is just starting to learn to reason. Like most of us, when we learn something new, we tend to forget it if we do not have a chance to master the skills.

Besides forming the right standards for your child, this also keeps him inquisitive so that he learns to ask questions and is learning all the time. Imagine if one asked questions and only got pacifying answers. After a while, one would give up asking particularly when one is at a stage of not knowing whether it is right to ask! Learning is a lifelong process. Encourage children to ask questions. Develop his inquisitiveness. Provide him with a standard that you think and know is right. Teach him morals and ethics. Ask him questions to think about and expand his mind and his horizons so he will not be timid, shy, and afraid to ask questions. Show him. Put actions into whatever you preach, he will model you.

By the time your child reaches school age (five or six years old), he is ready to go out into a world of strangers to start practicing and testing what he learned at home. He is ready to practice his technique of human relationships with persons other than family members under the guidance of a new authority, the teacher.

Typically a first grader comes home excited, yelling "mommy, mommy, you don't know. My teacher tells me such and such and this should be done this way!" Mothers and fathers no longer know everything. No matter what your background is, to the child the teacher is now the authority, the new standard. If your child has a problem, he can get the teacher to solve it or teach him how to solve it. Your child starts to question your authority, the standards you taught him during the formative years.

The teacher wants to teach your child to be a happy, healthy, well-adjusted, successful person. A teacher's goal is similar to a parent's goal. Yet, the teacher needs to obtain specifics from the parents: when not to contradict a parent and how to facilitate the parent's teaching at home. You can get involved in parent/teacher associations and classroom visitations. Let the teacher know what you want for your specific child. The child will get one standard instead of being confused. Worst of all, during this stage of development, there are many different influences that can modify the standards that children learn at home. Classmates at school, baby-sitters, caregivers, grandparents, and the like, all influence the growing child. Anything anywhere may be a new experience for your child. If, on the same issue, mother says one thing, teacher says another, baby-sitter says the third, and grandmother says she doesn't know. Who would we expect the child to follow? The child will probably do what is most convenient at that moment and learn to argue with you or he will be totally confused. Worse still, we say one thing and then do another. Your child observes this and this silently tears down the values that he has formed.

The latency period is a period of maturity. Children shed their childish innocence to mature under the guidance of a teacher. A primary school is a protected society where the young ones learn to interact with other people, with a mixture of different standards and from all walks of life. These standards are formed in a miniature form amongst our children and exhibited in the school with the teacher acting as a judge, authority, and guidance counselor. Through these contacts, children learn how to interact with people. They learn good and bad, right and wrong, and acceptance and rejection in a protected environment. We should make a coordinated effort to share our ideas and standards with teachers so they understand the master plan for our particular child. With this open communication between you and your child's teachers, your child faces consistency everywhere. There will not be any confusion, misunderstanding, mixed or double standards encountered. "Thou shall not steal" will be carried out no matter what it is or when it is. This sets the stage for the adolescent to be able to face challenges and improve our established standards.

Adolescence is an age of challenge. A typical adolescent will argue and fight with the establishment, be it the family, the school, or society. They try to push aside the previous standards and reestablish a new era, the adolescent's new world. Parents, teachers, and law enforcement officers often view this stage as threatening. Yet, this is a very positive stage of psychological development, provided we have been consistent during the previous stages. Just imagine if we had not challenged our forefathers, we would still be in the Stone Age. We would not have our civilization or our modern conveniences. The only difference between human beings and other mammals is that we challenge our superiors while other mammals do not. The cows stay in the fields forever because they do not challenge their forefathers and are content with what they are being taught. They are waiting in the fields to be slaughtered.

A teenager calls parents all kinds of names: you are dumb, stupid, do not understand teenagers, old fashioned, foolish, etc. A teenager knows everything and has a ready answer for any question and every uncertainty. Yet, he still likes to be bailed out of situations that he does not know how to handle. He relies on the fact that most parents still want to "baby them." He wants to manipulate and create situations where he can win. Parents always fall into this trap and find it frustrating and hard to deal with these situations. Yet, this is a fun age if we follow the basic principles of child psychology. You should establish your guidelines, accept him as an individual, give him liberties to choose, and let him bear his own responsibilities and natural consequences for his actions. He learns and matures into adulthood with the experiences he gains during these years.

Teenagers like to associate with their peers, yet they struggle to obtain their own identity. They yearn for their image and recognition by society. They dare to risk, to challenge, to disrupt routine, and to make a statement to get attention. It is all right to let them do so as long as they bear the responsibility and take the consequences.

Parents need to learn to avoid direct conflict with teenagers as long as they do not interfere with your rights. Their looks, their clothes, their hairstyles, and their companions are their choices and their liberty as long as they do not interfere with your adult world. However, when they start to disrupt your routine, they should be told and given reasons and choices to correct the situation or accept the responsibility for the direct result of such actions.

For example, a sixteen-year-old gets his driver's license, goes to a party and celebrates with his friends, gets drunk, and on the way home is picked up by a policeman and thrown in jail. This is not an uncommon scene in our society. The teenager calls home, his parents come and bail him out of jail, scold him a little, and ground him for a period of time. Before too long, he repeats the same scene again. Sure the parents know they cannot lock up their sixteen year old son. It was his choice to drink and no one forced him to swallow if he decided not to, yet no one can tape his mouth closed if he decides and he wants to do otherwise. It is up to him not to drink and drive at the same time. He deserves his jail sentence which is the natural consequence of what he chose to do. Yes, as a parent, you love him. The only way to prevent him from being locked up again is to go and visit him, to show him that you care about him and love him; but do not bail him out of jail. Otherwise, it becomes your sentence instead of his, and he knows that the next time around, he can expect the same thing - a telephone call will get him out, no big deal.

During this stage of development, parents are urged to accept him, give him liberty, and, at the same time, allow him to bear responsibilities. Accept your adolescent for who he is. Remember, you formed his morals and now you guide him with those moral principles. If you do not accept him as he is, you force him to jump the fence and run away. Give him his liberty to choose and let him have the results and consequences of his choices.

Planning

Parents are human beings, too. At times, we lose our perspective. Thus it is important to write out a plan for each child that is as detailed as possible to remind us during our frustrated times how to stay cool and follow our "blue print" to guide our children.

For us to put things into perspective, first we need to define the meaning of life and what we, as parents, want out of that particular life. The "do's and don'ts," the "good" and "bad," the "rights" and "wrongs," the "acceptable" and the "unacceptable," are all outlined and defined with particular references to the good qualities from the parents that we want to preserve and pass along to the next generation. Also, discuss the bad habits you possess that you want to shed, your goals in life and how to achieve them, your fears and the things and events you want to avoid in your child's life. Be specific and outline as many details as you can, based on the psychosocial development of the child, utilizing techniques like anticipatory guidance, positive reinforcement, and behavior modification in the formation of personality. Define the moral and ethical standards both parents will accept and preach as well as carrying out yourselves to avoid double standards in the eyes of your children. These areas are followed by providing a consistent environment during the latency years that leads to the teenage transformations and challenges to maturity.

In formulating the plan, one should emphasize the concept of family. "Do what is the best for the family," rather than "Do what is best for my baby" because the baby is always a "subset" of the family. If a parent suffers through sacrifice, eventually the baby suffers. The baby needs to adapt to the postnatal life: the baby needs to adapt to the family. This postnatal adaptation takes time and effort. The parents should be aware of it and work with their newborn.

This plan will be the most powerful tool in forming the new family, eventually society, and the world. Guess who will plan to have a son or daughter in jail twenty years down the road? Thus twenty years later, we will empty all our jails. Who wants to be unemployed? If we taught our children to enjoy working and learn how to create work for themselves, we would not have seven million unemployed. Nor do we want to have four generations of welfare recipients and seven trillion dollars' worth of national debt. As these social consequences are done by us, members of society, we can plan to undo them. If every member in society starts to think in these terms, plan in this fashion, and guide our next generation, we can overcome the social ills of our time. Why the arms race? Why "star wars"? Why can we not demonstrate that we can control and create our future based on our morals and ethics? We can show other people that the ways we create our new family, our new society, is a better way than self-destruction and nuclear holocaust.

This "blue print" concept will serve as the "immunization" against all social ills, just as vaccination eradicated the smallpox virus from our planet Earth. We build our children with good self-image, self-respect, confidence, and self-esteem to withstand temptations and manipulations. We develop their morals and ethics so that they understand right from wrong, good from bad, and the acceptable from the unacceptable. We provide ourselves as examples and models. They find consistency in their rules and regulations - the same rules that their parents and elders follow. We give them opportunities to seek adventure, to mature, to accept responsibility, and to bear the consequences of their choices.

Communication with Your Child

Open communication between you and your child is another important concept. You should be as open to your child as possible with regards to your child-rearing principles. Children like role models and they will learn at an early age. If you have some habits (drinking alcohol, smoking) that you do not necessarily want your child to learn, please do not do them in front of your child particularly during childhood. Otherwise, he will learn by your example and feel that he should do what his parents do. If possible, do not argue with your spouse openly in front of your child. It is common for your child to feel that he caused the argument and he will become depressed. He may take sides and aggravate the other parent. This can be avoided by settling the argument in private or when the children are asleep or off doing something elsewhere.

When your child asks you questions, try your best to answer them. If you do not know the answer, you can simply tell him that you do not know and request him to find the answer. This will stimulate him to learn in a positive fashion. You can, of course, try to find out the answer and then explain it to him. Please do not get angry with him and tell him not to ask questions. If this happens frequently, it will impair his willingness to learn and be inquisitive in the future.

Set achievable goals for your child so he has something to work on. However, be realistic with your goals. Your child will not feel frustrated by achievable goals. Praise your child if he is good. Console him if he feels disappointed when he cannot achieve what he should. You can tell him that you are unhappy if he fails to try, but not if he tries and fails.

You need to set limits for your child. Certainly indicate to him that if he exceeds the limits, he will be punished. Be consistent with your punishments. This means that both parents should do the same thing if the child exceeds the limit. He should always be punished for exceeding the limit even under special situations, like Christmas, New Year's, or in front of grandparents. Otherwise, he will learn that he can misbehave in certain circumstances. It is through this learning process that your child realizes there is law and order in society. You have to start this when he is young, even in the infancy period, so he learns consistently and early. Remember, these limits develop into your child's moral code, the code he will live by for the rest of his life.

If you have baby-sitters or other persons who share the care of your child, let them know your feelings and instruct them to do the same things you would do with your child. At least, have them report to you whatever they feel is out of bounds according to your limits.

Do not be afraid to discipline your children. Discipline is an act of love. You definitely would not want to discipline a stranger's child because you do not love him or care about him. Tell your child specifically why he deserves what he gets when he has done wrong. Also, tell him that you discipline him because you love him and you expect him to behave and obey. Explain to him the disappointment you feel when you have to invoke disciplinary action. Corporal punishment before the age three carries no lasting effect other than teaching your child to be violent. Typically, your two-year-old thinks that his parent is angry rather than that he is wrong and deserves to be punished. This is because he is still in the "amoral" stage of cognitive development. Punishment can be in the form of not allowing your child to watch television for a period of time or not allowing him to play outside, etc. Do not punish him by asking him to do household chores, reading, or writing. He will associate all of his work as punishment later in life and will consider them painful chores in daily life.

Involve your children in household work in a positive way. We want to clean the house because we enjoy cleanliness. Make sure that he understands that it is also his responsibility to keep the house clean and tidy. Do not pay him to do household work. Inform him that he is expected to do so because he is a member of the family. Encourage him to do voluntary work so this can build a positive image for him.

You should encourage your child to communicate with you freely. Do not discourage him from talking. Through what he tells you, you can understand what he thinks and how he feels. This free communication will avoid the so-called "generation gap" and prevent the undesirable, bad habits of child, for example, lies, drugs, and sex. He should feel free to say what he wants to say. You and he can have a civil debate over issues that you do not agree on. You can provide explanations and support for your arguments and you can ask for his documentation and support. It is through this democratic process that your youngster will excel in society.

Encourage your child to communicate with his doctor. He can ask his doctor any question, and his doctor will try his best to answer it. His doctor should respect him as an individual. Please expect his doctor to keep his professional confidentiality towards patients, even if the patient is your child. It is the only way for a doctor to establish rapport with his patients. He should receive special and individual attention as if he is the doctor's own child. Between the ages of seven and eight, you can expect your doctor to talk to your child about drugs, chemical abuse, and alcohol. Drug and alcohol abuse plagues our generation. It is estimated that 95% of all children have experienced drugs by the time they have graduated from high school. He will be told the effects of drug and alcohol abuse and the undesirable side effects of addiction. Your doctor will encourage your child not to use drugs or other chemicals. However, your child will make the final decision. Again, this depends on his upbringing, environment, moral standards, family support, and the communication between you and your child. Drugs, cigarettes, and alcohol are plentiful in any area of the United States. If your child wants to use drugs or alcohol, he can get them. However, if you start early in a preventative approach, you can be sure that your child will have the correct attitude towards drugs and choose what is right for him.

Your doctor may expect you to instruct your daughter between the ages of nine and ten on sexual development and menstruation, depending on her maturation. She should learn to accept menstruation in a positive way. It is physiological and there should be no shame or other misconceptions about menstruation. Moreover, it is a very scary experience for the young lady to have her first period unprepared, for example, at school or in camp where she may receive unnecessary negative comments or be ridiculed. Talk to her about personal hygiene during her periods, about the unusual feelings she may experience, and at times, the lower abdominal pain or other symptoms. These symptoms should be reported immediately to you. Proper sex education should be taught to your child early to avoid unnecessary misconception or self exploration in sex. Inform her how babies are conceived and developed, and, through a continuous process, how the baby is born. Nationally, statistics show that about 65% of girls have their first sexual intercourse before they graduate from high school. Be prepared to explain to her at an early age that sexual relationships mean responsibilities. She should realize that she may bear children and have a responsibility to the next generation. Before she is sexually active, she should know about contraceptive methods. Your doctor may not prescribe contraceptives because of religious reasons. Your doctor should refer her to a gynecologist or to your family doctor. It is also important that she should have a yearly gynecological examination if she is sexually active. If you do not feel that you can vocalize all these facts to your daughter, your doctor should be willing to do that counseling for you. Other alternatives would be talking to your pastor or attending a Planned Parenthood service. They can give her appropriate answers and counseling.

Boys normally mature later. Your doctor expects you to give sex education at home, similar to the information you give your daughter. National statistics for boys show that 75% of them have their first sexual intercourse before they graduate high school. Again, they should realize how babies are conceived and the responsibilities involved in bringing up a family. Emphasize the responsibilities of being a father.

Practically all children masturbate. It is normal for them to explore their bodies and find pleasure in fondling themselves. Do not humiliate your child. However, if he masturbates excessively, it usually indicates that some psychopathology exists. You should ask him specifically about this or have his doctor talk to him if you do not feel comfortable addressing these issues with your child.

Parenting Skills

Parenting is an underdeveloped skill. There is no formal training. Traditionally, this skill is passed from generation to generation through observation, coaching, and direct modeling. In a fast moving, capitalistic society like the United States of America, most parents find it difficult to learn a new set of skills to nurture their children. However, these skills are essential to successful child rearing in the twenty-first century. We cannot rely on the old methods our forefathers passed on in our democratic society. Moreover, society cannot afford all the currents ills and be able to sustain and thrive in the future. We want our children to grow up in a happy, healthy, peaceful and productive society. We want to overcome the current social injustice and disharmony in our country.

Parenting skills are learned skills. With commitments from the parents and the guiding principles of our forefathers and our religious beliefs, we can establish utopia on earth.

The following skills are widely utilized by clinical psychologists. These skills are taught in graduate level classes, seminars, and continuing education courses for counselors, psychologists, social workers, and teachers. It is important for people to learn these skills even before they consider having children! These skills should be taught in junior high and high schools as a required course for graduation.

Mutual Respect

Respect is mutual. Respect is earned. Learn to respect your child, starting in infancy. When your infant enters the world, he learns to adapt to his postnatal life. There are a lot of adjustments for him to make! It is up

211

to you to appreciate his effort of learning and adjusting. You truly need to respect his efforts, from learning to eat, to communicating with you, to sleeping independently, and most of all, to tolerating his own frustrations. Any newborn would want to go back inside his mother's womb, if possible. Thus, simulating the in-utero environments, like a soothing rhythm, a rocking motion, or cuddling him, will calm a fussy newborn. You need to learn to respect his efforts by providing a nurturing environment all the time. He will learn to respect you and your efforts. As your child grows, you need to maintain this mutual respect, and he will learn to respect you. By providing him with explanations and reasons, he grows to learn to accept logical consequences and become an ethical person. You should never belittle your child and his feelings. You will lose his respect for you if you do not respect him. He is, after all, as much a human being as any one of us. He deserves respect.

Consistency

Your child must clearly understand what is expected of him before he can learn to adjust his behavior to suit your requirements. Communicate with your child consistently, by your words, your gestures, and your actions. Your child is modeling you and learning from you all the time. You are his idol and his model. You have to live by your own rules consistently, and your child will learn. Yes, your youngster will break the rules and test your response. Be consistent. The same rules should apply to your child as they apply to your spouse! Your child will learn that there is only one standard. He is an equal member in the family as well as in his society. This same standard applies equally to him and everyone else. This concept of consistency also applies in all special conditions, like holidays, vacations, grandparents visiting, celebrations, parties, etc. When your youngster sees that there are no exceptions under any situation, he will learn to accept the facts that all members of the family live by the same rules.

Natural Consequences

Natural consequences are not punishments. No one can or is able to change nature's consequences. When your child touches something hot, his hand will be burned. Yes, you can teach your child the concept of pain when he touches hot substances; however, if he still decides to touch the hot stove, he will experience pain. You cannot alter this natural consequence. Let nature takes its course. Natural consequences is a very powerful parenting tool. You do not need to preach, persuade, scream, or be angry. Your child will learn. He will not touch a hot stove again, possibly for his lifetime! He may also be able to generalize this concept that hot water may scald causing pain, too! The concept of "hot" will be ingrained in his mind. Within reason, you should let nature does its wonders. However, some common sense applies. You cannot let your youngster be run over by an automobile, just to let him experience the consequence! You should always try to avoid serious, harmful, dangerous accidents.

Logical Consequences

Logical consequences work wonders, too, just like natural consequences. Be logical so that your youngster can associate what he has done with the consequence. Logical consequences can be applied to any child after the age of five to six when he enters the latency stage of his development. He will learn the logic and the consequence behind his actions. When he fails to hand in his homework on time, he will get detention and have to walk home because he missed his school bus or his ride home! When he doodles in the morning, he will have to go to school in his pajamas, and be there the whole day ridiculed by his classmates. You do not need to rescue him in these situations. You did not cause these consequences. He decides to experience them. He is in control. He can modify his behavior the next time and learn from the consequences. You respect him. You love him. You let him make his decisions. These are his choices and his decisions, and he gets the logical consequences. On the other hand, if you do not respect him and try to bail him out, you will find that he enjoys the attention he gets in his class when you bring in his homework. He will be the "class's hero" because he demonstrated to his classmates how he can manipulate a powerful adult. Since there is no consequence for him, he will not learn. You will be bringing in his homework often until you get angry, losing your respect for him as a competent individual.

"I" Messages

"I" messages consist of four parts. It begins with "when you do such and such," followed by "your feeling," then you give your reason, like "because you have done something wrong," then you provide an alternative, like "I would rather you do such and such" to complete your message. You will find that this message is powerful in directing your child's behavior. Basically, your child wants to please you, get your attention, and positively interact with you. Unfortunately, he may not know how to do that. It is so much easier for your child to get your negative attention than to get your positive attention! Your child misbehaves for a reason. He wants your attention. Just imagine how often in the course of a day you stroke your child's head and lovingly tell him that he is doing a great job playing by himself and how often you scream "no, no!" At him? "I" messages will teach your child about your feelings, your reasoning, and your preference. He will learn. "I" messages redirect his subconscious intent of getting your attention in a new, positive way. With practice, you will master this technique of delivering a lesson to your child. Your child will learn to be a logical, ethical person with sound reasoning and an even temper, modeling you!

Reflection

Children observe and learn. They act to obtain their desired goals, even though at times, their goals may be misguided. Children are deliberate and persistent. They devise new and effective ways to achieve their desires. They want to get your attention and evade unpleasant duties and obligations. You can use the skill of reflection. Repeat what your child just said or did, showing him exactly what occurred. You reflect like a mirror. This technique is particularly useful in attempting to understand your child. By repeating what he said, you make him think about the content of what he said and ponder it. You can add your feelings and comments about his statement. Let him take time to respond. Reflection requires your patience. You are calm and act deliberately. You are not reacting to his statement. By paraphrasing his words, you guide him to think about what he has just said or done. When you add your feelings and comments to his response of your reflection, you teach him that he should respect you, just like you respect him. He will learn. Reflection is not a punishment. It is an important teaching technique. A related skill is called reflective listening. Reflective listening is also a powerful communication tool. It teaches your child to clarify his words and his comments, communicating his feelings so that you and his peers can understand him. He will learn the technique of reflection, benefiting him in the future.

Restraint

Children need love, guidance, encouragement, stimulation, and tenderness. They need your attention; in particular, your positive attention. You also need to let your child learn, using the principles of natural and logical consequences, to help your child become a successful, independent individual. You need to learn to restrain yourself from providing uninvited comments or advice. When you utilize the technique of restraint, you need to be observant. You should restrain from making any negative comments about his actions. You should guide him positively, showing him that he can perform. He will learn. By providing opportunities for him to learn from your positive guidance, he will build his self-confidence and march forward into maturity. The technique of restraint will transform your child from an irresponsible person into an independent human being with a matured sense of self-respect and responsibility. With your trust and love, he will feel encouraged and be stimulated to learn. You refrain from limiting his learning potential through natural and logical consequences. Your child will assume a lot of his duties at an early age. It is his duty to learn to be independent and to communicate with you. He can carry out his duties. Restrain from "babying" him!

Curiosity

Children are naturally curious. They want to learn. They want to explore their environment. By utilizing their curiosity, you can capture their attention, creating a new learning experience for them. Children act with a purpose. They expect a certain reaction from you. When you act in the opposite way of what they expect, they lose their balance and wonder what you are doing. You can redirect your child's misbehavior by acting the opposite way from what he is expecting. He feels strange. He loses his balance and control. On the other hand, you provoke his curiosity. He wants to know what you may do next. You can deliver a message of your feelings, your guidance, and your reasoning. Your child will listen and learn. You can detect what your child expects by observing your child and noting what your normal reaction would be. Your own reaction normally reflects your child's expectation. By doing something that he does not expect, this arouses his curiosity. He becomes attentive, wanting to see what comes next! Instead of falling into your child's trap, you have created a positive learning experience for him. It is through his curiosity that he learns, becomes innovative, and successful in his future.

Instill Confidence

A self-confident child is a successful person. With your teaching and guidance, he will develop his self-confidence. You will nurture this virtue by respecting him, his decisions, and his actions. Let natural and logical consequences work their wonders. If you are committed to these principles of child rearing, you will gain your child's confidence. Naturally, you love your child. By your genuine benevolence and tenderness, your child will perceive your unconditional trust. Indulgence on your part will not gain your child's confidence. Permissiveness will not impress him as good will. You want him to think and act independently, knowing that you can trust him to make the right decisions. You can gain his trust by playing with him, talking to him, expressing your feelings towards him, and positively interacting with him. If you trust him, you will earn his trust in return. He knows that your genuine love for him will help him grow up to be a successful, independent person. Your actions are far more effective than your flattery or empty praises. Your actions speak a lot louder than any of your words.

Encouragement

Children need courage to learn and grow to be successful adults. They need to venture into territories of unknown waters, making decisions on their way, similar to explorers trying to find new trails. They need your encouragement. Your child needs your help to guide him. But, he needs to learn to decide for himself. A loving mother will nurture and commend her child's efforts, trusting that he will be able to do a good job. It takes courage on the mother's part to let her child experiment and try, letting natural and logical consequences work. Your unsolicited help will be a hindrance to his learning, tearing down his confidence and his courage. He will feel degraded by your "kindness." Your child should be commended for what he has done and his attempts to do something, not for what he is. No matter what your child's failing, you can bring about an improvement through encouragement. It may be easier, faster, or better when you try to "help" your child to do a certain task. However, you take away his courage to attempt to do the task, the accompanying experience he may gain, and his self-reliance. He feels defeated and useless in that situation and has doubts about himself. You may help him, teach him, and guide him when he requests your input; however, your unsolicited intrusion destroys his confidence and discourages him.

Withdrawal

Children behave for a reason; they act for the adults who are present in their environment. Even Mike Tyson will not fight without an audience! Your child is no different. He acts for you, consciously or subconsciously. By withdrawing yourself from the situation, you will find dramatic results that you may not expect. If you refuse to play the role of "super-hero," your child will learn to overcome his weakness and learn to perform the required functions. A "dependent" child is usually a "demanding" child. A "disobedient" child is normally a "tyrannical" child. When you retreat into you own comfortable zone, like your bedroom, you will find that harmony will soon appear. This normally occurs after a brief period of protest with crying and banging the door. You may then emerge as a warm, loving mother again.

Withdrawal differs from neglect. You should never neglect your child. However, when you feel that you are tired of rendering services to your child, serving your child constantly, you should retreat. You are not his maid! When you refuse to perform the service, out of necessity he will learn to do it. After all, he learned to eat, walk, and talk! A word of caution, you should "baby proof" and "poison proof" your home before you utilize the technique of withdrawal.

Request

Children demand dignity. They are your equal. You should respect your child if you want to gain his respect. He must learn to control himself, by himself alone. You respect him by providing a nurturing environment in your home for him to learn. You guide him. However, you cannot force him or coerce him to learn. Even though "reward" and "punishment" are used extensively by parents as child rearing skills, these techniques are harmful because they are only expressions of assumed parental authority. When you treat and respect your child as an equal human being, you earn his trust and confidence in you. If you openly discuss and analyze certain situation with him, making your request rather than delivering a command, you will gain cooperation and be successful most of the time. He will see that it is for the common good to perform and fulfill your request. Keep your request simple, with an adequate explanation of the request so that your child can understand and follow it. Avoid delivering several requests at the same time. Your child may feel overwhelmed. Always be thankful and commend him on his efforts so that he feels he is appreciated. You requests will enhance his self-confidence and foster his self-image at the same time. Refrain from making negative comments. You should try to teach the correct procedures, rather than correcting wrong ones. Let natural or logical consequences speak for you.

Motivation

Children do not want to sit and stare. They want action. It is up to their parents to channel their children's energy in a positive way. Positively motivating your child is an important skill you should master, even when your child is still an infant. After all, he will need to learn to effectively communicate with you. Ever since his conception, he has been totally dependent on you. He would like for that to continue. However, as a parent, your goal may be a little different. You want him to grow up to be an independent individual, successful in society. You need him to learn to take the steps to achieve his goals. You need to teach him to set goals for himself. For example, if he does not want to spend time looking for his toys when he needs them, he learns to pick them up after playing with them, and store them in a place where he knows how to find them. Natural and logical consequences are good self-motivating tools. If he wants to be successful, be it in school or sports, he will learn to put his effort into reading and practice. You need to guide your child to be self-motivated, knowing that he will make the final decision to perform for himself, for you, for your family, and for society. A good method of motivating your child is to let him learn to decide for himself. You can explore options with him, brainstorming, and discussing various options. He has to be the person to decide which course he wants to take. When he sees the results of his decision, both positive and negative, he learns. Since none of us are perfect, it is absolutely all right to let your youngster make decisions that may not be your choice. He will learn from the mistakes he makes, and learn to avoid them the next time around. Please do not stifle your child's decision making-skills and self-motivation with your "good intentions."

Discipline

Discipline is an act of love. You care about your child; you love your child. You want to guide your child to do the right thing at the right time. Children learn. They learn and model you all the time. By providing your child with what he truly needs at the time, you teach him communication skills and let him learn the consequences of ineffective communication. You will not spoil your child by giving him too much attention. He deserves your attention as much as you deserve your child's attention. On the other hand, you should not let your child manipulate you. You should set your standards, your routines, and let your child know what you expect. He will learn. When your baby cries, find out the meaning of his cry. If he has a good reason, he deserves the consequences of communicating with you. If he does not have a good reason to cry - he has been fed, his diaper is clean, and he is warm and comfortable, it is perfectly all right to let him learn to tolerate his frustration. He will learn the consequences of ineffective communication.

Discipline is teaching. You should set limits for your family. You should also follow these limits as you are a member of your family. If you stretch or bend the limits for you or your spouse, your child will learn to do the same, testing your limits. Be consistent. Consistency teaches your child what to expect under any situation. Develop a set of routines for your child and your family. Your child will learn your routines.

When your child learns to communicate with you verbally, you should encourage him to tell you how he feels and what he thinks about his requests and his desires. He should also give you the reasons and logic behind his requests. You should let him know how you feel and what you think about the situation, explaining your reasoning and logic about the effects of his requests and desires. He will learn to be assertive, thinking for himself and for others prior to his actions in the future.

Physical punishments like spanking, hitting, or shaking your child are not discipline. You are teaching your child to be violent. "When I am angry, I can hit people." What your child perceives when you spank him or hit him is: "mommy is angry and she hits me." Most of the time, your child may not know what he has done to deserve your anger. Instead, try to explain to your child what happened and how you feel about the incident. Suggest to him an alternative solution to the problem. He will learn if you are calm and serene. If you respect him and his dignity, he will respect you.

There are many other skills and techniques that you can learn and adapt to your family's situation. It is important to remember your goal as a parent. You want to raise a happy, healthy, well-adjusted, responsible, ethical and successful individual who is a pillar of the future society.

part

Emergencies

Please call the office telephone number, which is answered night and day for non-life threatening emergencies. For life threatening emergencies, dial 911, and the emergency medical service will respond, and the emergency medical technicians will stabilize the condition and transport the victim to the nearest medical facility for further care and contact your doctor.

If the situation is not urgent, please call first, for your doctor may well be at one of the hospitals, unable to leave, and could have you meet him or her there. On normal office days, your doctor may try to return calls between 1 o'clock and 2 o'clock, the lunch hour, or after 6 o'clock in the evening.

Sick Visits

When your child is sick, your doctor expects you to call the office, which should have a twenty four hour a day answering service, or even the doctor's home if necessary. Your doctor will try his or her best to see them as soon as possible. Most doctors prefer scheduled appointments, yet if the available appointments are fully booked, just bring your child in the office and most of the time your doctor will take care of your child. Be understanding in that in such instances you will be expected to wait a little longer. Scheduling helps to cut down the waiting time in the office and also cuts down the cross infections between your child and other children in the office. Thus, scheduled patients will have priority. However, if an emergency arises, your doctor will definitely attend to the emergency situation first. This rule applies to your child as well as others. This is in accord with the code of medical ethics.

Through the continuing medical education process, your doctor will keep updated with new medical knowledge. He or she will explain to you the basis of pathophysiology involved in the care of your child's sickness, both physically and emotionally.

If your child has a sore throat, expect your doctor to do a throat culture to rule out the possibility of streptococcus infection. It has been estimated that 85% - 95% of all sore throat infections are viral in origin. Symptomatic relief of their fever and sore throat is all that is necessary. In this case penicillin will do more harm than good. However if the culture results indicate the pathogenic strains of streptococcus, your doctor will need to administer an antibiotic to your child to eradicate the bacteria and prevent complications of the disease. Penicillin will not control the fever and the sore throat. Again, symptomatic treatment will take care of the sore throat and the fever. Often an ear infection accompanies a sore throat, your doctor, therefore, will check your child's ears.

If your child develops a wax build-up in his or her ear canal, expect your doctor to clean them out and examine their ear drums to rule out ear infections. Your doctor will not guess what hides behind the wax and prescribe an antibiotic to treat a fever. Antibiotics are potent medications and are reserved for specific treatment of bacterial infections. Do not expect your doctor to prescribe an antibiotic over the phone because he or she cannot consciously examine your child adequately over the phone. Some State Board of Medical Examiners considers telephone prescriptions do not meet the standard of care. Your doctor will be held accountable for not meeting the standard!

Physicians do not believe in magic cures, and the disease process will run a normal course of events, hopefully with complete recovery at the end. Your "twenty-four hour flu" or the "three day measles" are examples of them. Experimental settings prove that penicillin will not shorten the course of a streptococcal infection. The number of days of fever, the degrees of soreness in the throat, as well as difficultly in swallowing, all remained statistically the same despite of early or late treatment of the disease. This phenomenon can easily be explained by an example. A simple cut of the skin, whether infected or not, will take time to heal. Similarly, once inflammation sets in the throat, it will take time to heal, whether or not it is infected with bacteria or viruses. Please do not expect your child to feel better immediately after being seen by your doctor. The disease process will take time to heal. Modern medicine may hasten the healing process, but there is no magic cure.

If your child has a complicated disease, expect your doctor to consult other physicians. Pediatricians generally do not do surgery. If surgery is necessary, your doctor will consult the surgeon who he feels is the best qualified to do that specific operation, and your doctor will explain the situation to you. Sometimes your doctor may let you choose your own surgeon, at other times; he may recommend one to you because your doctor feels that particular surgeon is best for your child. Your doctor will seek the best available local help first. If they are not available, your doctor may refer you to an out-of-town physician for consultation and you may have some input to where will be more convenient for you and your family. Communicate with your doctor freely. Express your fear and your concern. Your doctor will find the best way to serve you and your child's needs.

If you feel that your doctor is not managing your child appropriately let your doctor know. If you decide to seek a second opinion, talk to your doctor and normally he will recommend someone for you. It is hopeful that your doctor stays as objective as possible as any physician; however, your doctor may be biased in certain areas. Communicate freely with your doctor. Your doctor should not feel offended and will try his best to seek the appropriate physician for your child and your situation.

Office Waiting Time

Your doctor will make every attempt to see you at your appointed time. However, during peak illness seasons or when emergencies occur, you may have to wait for extended periods of time. The office staff will be able to explain and apologize for such inconveniences. The delays are usually the result of sick children being worked into the schedule or some form of emergency.

Your doctor may share night and week-end calls with his associates so that a doctor is available to answer your questions or see your child if it is necessary at all times. During office hours your doctor will return your calls. Please do not hesitate to call if you have concerns regarding your child.

Recommended Childhood and Adolescent Immunization Schedule

Vaccine ▼ Age ▶	Birth	1 month	2 months	4 months	6 months
Hepatitis B[1]	HepB #1	///////// HepB #2			▓▓▓
Diphtheria, Tetanus, Pertussis[2]			DTaP	DTaP	DTaP
Haemophilus influenzae type b[3]			Hib	Hib	Hib
Inactivated Poliovirus			IPV	IPV	▓▓▓
Measles, Mumps, Rubella[4]					
Varicella[5]					
Pneumococcal[6]			PCV	PCV	PCV
Influenza[7]					▓▓▓
· — · — · — · — · — · Vaccines below red line are for selected populations · — ·						
Hepatitis A[8]					

This schedule indicates the recommended ages for routine administration of currently licensed childhood vaccines, as of December 1, 2004, for children through age 18 years. Any dose not administered at the recommended age should be administered at any subsequent visit when indicated and feasible.

▓▓▓ Indicates age groups that warrant special effort to administer those vaccines not previously administered. Additional vaccines may be licensed and recommended during the year. Licensed combination vaccines may be used whenever any components of the combination are indicated and other components of the vaccine

DEPARTMENT OF HEALTH AND HUMAN SERVICES
CENTERS FOR DISEASE CONTROL AND PREVENTION

United States • 2005

12 months	15 months	18 months	24 months	4–6 years	11–12 years	13–18 years
HepB #3			HepB Series			
	DTaP			DTaP	Td	Td
Hib						
IPV				IPV		
MMR #1				MMR #2		MMR #2
Varicella				Varicella		
PCV			PCV	PPV		
Influenza (Yearly)			Influenza (Yearly)			
				Hepatitis A Series		

are not contraindicated. Providers should consult the manufacturers' package inserts for detailed recommendations. Clinically significant adverse events that follow immunization should be reported to the Vaccine Adverse Event Reporting System (VAERS). Guidance about how to obtain and complete a VAERS form are available at www.vaers.org or by telephone, 800-822-7967.

▒ Range of recommended ages   ▨ Only if mother HBsAg(–)

▒ Preadolescent assessment   ■ Catch-up immunization

The Childhood and Adolescent Immunization Schedule is approved by:
Advisory Committee on Immunization Practices www.cdc.gov/nip/acip
American Academy of Pediatrics www.aap.org
American Academy of Family Physicians www.aafp.org

Footnotes
Recommended Childhood and
Adolescent Immunization Schedule

1. **Hepatitis B (HepB) vaccine.** All infants should receive the first dose of HepB vaccine soon after birth and before hospital discharge; the first dose may also be administered by age 2 months if the mother is hepatitis B surface antigen (HBsAg) negative. Only monovalent HepB may be used for the birth dose. Monovalent or combination vaccine containing HepB may be used to complete the series. Four doses of vaccine may be administered when a birth dose is given. The second dose should be administered at least 4 weeks after the first dose, except for combination vaccines which cannot be administered before age 6 weeks. The third dose should be given at least 16 weeks after the first dose and at least 8 weeks after the second dose. The last dose in the vaccination series (third or fourth dose) should not be administered before age 24 weeks.

   Infants born to HBsAg-positive mothers should receive HepB and 0.5 mL of hepatitis B immune globulin (HBIG) at separate sites within 12 hours of birth. The second dose is recommended at age 1–2 months. The final dose in the immunization series should not be administered before age 24 weeks. These infants should be tested for HBsAg and antibody to HBsAg (anti-HBs) at age 9–15 months.

   Infants born to mothers whose HBsAg status is unknown should receive the first dose of the HepB series within 12 hours of birth. Maternal blood should be drawn as soon as possible to determine the mother's HBsAg status; if the HBsAg test is positive, the infant should receive HBIG as soon as possible (no later than age 1 week). The second dose is recommended at age 1–2 months. The last dose in the immunization series should not be administered before age 24 weeks.

2. **Diphtheria and tetanus toxoids and acellular pertussis (DTaP) vaccine.** The fourth dose of DTaP may be administered as early as age 12 months, provided 6 months have elapsed since the third dose and the child is unlikely to return at age 15–18 months. The final dose in the series should be given at age ≥4 years. **Tetanus and diphtheria toxoids (Td)** is recommended at age 11–12 years if at least 5 years have elapsed since the last dose of tetanus and diphtheria toxoid-containing vaccine. Subsequent routine Td boosters are recommended every 10 years.

3. ***Haemophilus influenzae* type b (Hib) conjugate vaccine.** Three Hib conjugate vaccines are licensed for infant use. If PRP-OMP (PedvaxHIB® or ComVax® [Merck]) is administered at ages 2 and 4 months, a dose at age 6 months is not required. DTaP/Hib combination products should not be used for primary immunization in infants at ages 2, 4 or 6 months but can be used as boosters after any Hib vaccine. The final dose in the series should be administered at age ≥12 months.

Footnotes
United States • 2005

4. Measles, mumps, and rubella vaccine (MMR). The second dose of MMR is recommended routinely at age 4–6 years but may be administered during any visit, provided at least 4 weeks have elapsed since the first dose and both doses are administered beginning at or after age 12 months. Those who have not previously received the second dose should complete the schedule by age 11–12 years.

5. Varicella vaccine. Varicella vaccine is recommended at any visit at or after age 12 months for susceptible children (i.e., those who lack a reliable history of chickenpox). Susceptible persons aged ≥13 years should receive 2 doses administered at least 4 weeks apart.

6. Pneumococcal vaccine. The heptavalent **pneumococcal conjugate vaccine (PCV)** is recommended for all children aged 2–23 months and for certain children aged 24–59 months. The final dose in the series should be given at age ≥12 months. **Pneumococcal polysaccharide vaccine (PPV)** is recommended in addition to PCV for certain high-risk groups. See *MMWR* 2000;49(RR-9):1-35.

7. Influenza vaccine. Influenza vaccine is recommended annually for children aged ≥6 months with certain risk factors (including, but not limited to, asthma, cardiac disease, sickle cell disease, human immunodeficiency virus [HIV], and diabetes), healthcare workers, and other persons (including household members) in close contact with persons in groups at high risk (see *MMWR* 2004;53[RR-6]:1-40). In addition, healthy children aged 6–23 months and close contacts of healthy children aged 0–23 months are recommended to receive influenza vaccine because children in this age group are at substantially increased risk for influenza-related hospitalizations. For healthy persons aged 5–49 years, the intranasally administered, live, attenuated influenza vaccine (LAIV) is an acceptable alternative to the intramuscular trivalent inactivated influenza vaccine (TIV). See *MMWR* 2004;53(RR-6):1-40. Children receiving TIV should be administered a dosage appropriate for their age (0.25 mL if aged 6–35 months or 0.5 mL if aged ≥3 years). Children aged ≤8 years who are receiving influenza vaccine for the first time should receive 2 doses (separated by at least 4 weeks for TIV and at least 6 weeks for LAIV).

8. Hepatitis A vaccine. Hepatitis A vaccine is recommended for children and adolescents in selected states and regions and for certain high-risk groups; consult your local public health authority. Children and adolescents in these states, regions, and high-risk groups who have not been immunized against hepatitis A can begin the hepatitis A immunization series during any visit. The 2 doses in the series should be administered at least 6 months apart. See *MMWR* 1999;48(RR-12):1-37.

Recommended Immunization Schedule for Children and Adolescents Who Start Late or Who Are More Than 1 Month Behind
UNITED STATES • 2005

The tables below give catch-up schedules and minimum intervals between doses for children who have delayed immunizations. There is no need to restart a vaccine series regardless of the time that has elapsed between doses. Use the chart appropriate for the child's age.

CATCH-UP SCHEDULE FOR CHILDREN AGED 4 MONTHS THROUGH 6 YEARS

Vaccine	Minimum Age for Dose 1	Minimum Interval Between Doses			
		Dose 1 to Dose 2	Dose 2 to Dose 3	Dose 3 to Dose 4	Dose 4 to Dose 5
Diphtheria, Tetanus, Pertussis	6 wks	4 weeks	4 weeks	6 months	6 months[1]
Inactivated Poliovirus	6 wks	4 weeks	4 weeks	4 weeks[2]	
Hepatitis B[3]	Birth	4 weeks	8 weeks (and 16 weeks after first dose)		
Measles, Mumps, Rubella	12 mo	4 weeks[4]			
Varicella	12 mo				
Haemophilus influenzae type b[5]	6 wks	4 weeks if first dose given at age <12 months; 8 weeks (as final dose) if first dose given at age 12–14 months; No further doses needed if first dose given at age ≥15 months	4 weeks[6] if current age <12 months; 8 weeks (as final dose)[6] if current age ≥12 months and second dose given at age <15 months; No further doses needed if previous dose given at age ≥15 mo	8 weeks (as final dose) This dose only necessary for children aged 12 months–5 years who received 3 doses before age 12 months	
Pneumococcal[7]	6 wks	4 weeks if first dose given at age <12 months and current age <24 months; 8 weeks (as final dose) if first dose given at age ≥12 months or current age 24–59 months; No further doses needed for healthy children if first dose given at age ≥24 months	4 weeks if current age <12 months; 8 weeks (as final dose) if current age ≥12 months; No further doses needed for healthy children if previous dose given at age ≥24 months	8 weeks (as final dose) This dose only necessary for children aged 12 months–5 years who received 3 doses before age 12 months	

CATCH-UP SCHEDULE FOR CHILDREN AGED 7 YEARS THROUGH 18 YEARS

Vaccine	Minimum Interval Between Doses		
	Dose 1 to Dose 2	Dose 2 to Dose 3	Dose 3 to Booster Dose
Tetanus, Diphtheria	4 weeks	6 months	**6 months[8]** if first dose given at age <12 months and current age <11 years **5 years[8]** if first dose given at age ≥12 months and third dose given at age <7 years and current age ≥11 years **10 years[8]** if third dose given at age ≥7 years
Inactivated Poliovirus[9]	4 weeks	4 weeks	IPV[2,9]
Hepatitis B	4 weeks	8 weeks (and 16 weeks after first dose)	
Measles, Mumps, Rubella	4 weeks		
Varicella[10]	4 weeks		

Children and Adolescents Catch-up Schedules   UNITED STATES • 2005

Footnotes

1. **DTaP.** The fifth dose is not necessary if the fourth dose was administered after the fourth birthday.
2. **IPV.** For children who received an all-IPV or all-oral poliovirus (OPV) series, a fourth dose is not necessary if third dose was administered at age ≥4 years. If both OPV and IPV were administered as part of a series, a total of 4 doses should be given, regardless of the child's current age.
3. **HepB.** All children and adolescents who have not been immunized against hepatitis B should begin the HepB immunization series during any visit. Providers should make special efforts to immunize children who were born in, or whose parents were born in, areas of the world where hepatitis B virus infection is moderately or highly endemic.
4. **MMR.** The second dose of MMR is recommended routinely at age 4–6 years but may be administered earlier if desired.
5. **Hib.** Vaccine is not generally recommended for children aged ≥5 years.
6. **Hib.** If current age <12 months and the first 2 doses were PRP-OMP (PedvaxHIB® or ComVax® [Merck]), the third (and final) dose should be administered at age 12–15 months and at least 8 weeks after the second dose.
7. **PCV.** Vaccine is not generally recommended for children aged ≥5 years.
8. **Td.** For children aged 7–10 years, the interval between the third and booster dose is determined by the age when the first dose was administered. For adolescents aged 11–18 years, the interval is determined by the age when the third dose was given.
9. **IPV.** Vaccine is not generally recommended for persons aged ≥18 years.
10. **Varicella.** Administer the 2-dose series to all susceptible adolescents aged ≥13 years.

Report adverse reactions to vaccines through the federal Vaccine Adverse Event Reporting System. For information on reporting reactions following immunization, please visit www.vaers.org or call the 24-hour national toll-free information line 800-822-7967. Report suspected cases of vaccine-preventable diseases to your state or local health department.

For additional information about vaccines, including precautions and contraindications for immunization and vaccine shortages, please visit the National Immunization Program Web site at www.cdc.gov/nip or call the National Immunization Information Hotline at 800-232-2522 (English) or 800-232-0233 (Spanish).

Birth to 36 months: Boys
Length-for-age and Weight-for-age percentiles

NAME _____

RECORD # _____

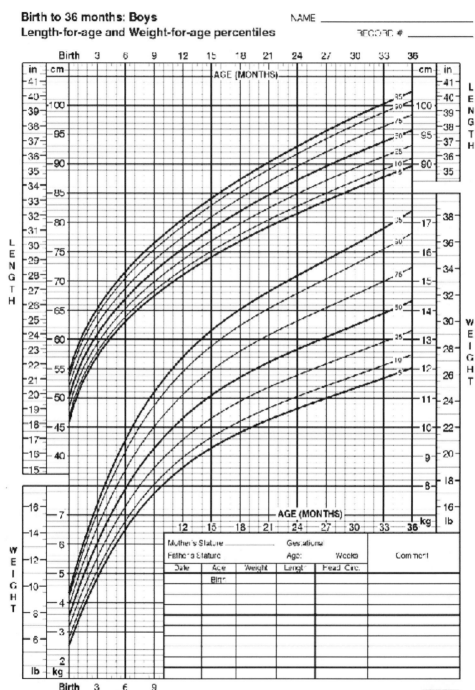

Published May 30, 2000 (modified 4/20/01).
SOURCE: Developed by the National Center for Health Statistics in collaboration with
the National Center for Chronic Disease Prevention and Health Promotion (2000).
http://www.cdc.gov/growthcharts

Birth to 36 months: Girls
Length-for-age and Weight-for-age percentiles

NAME

RECORD #

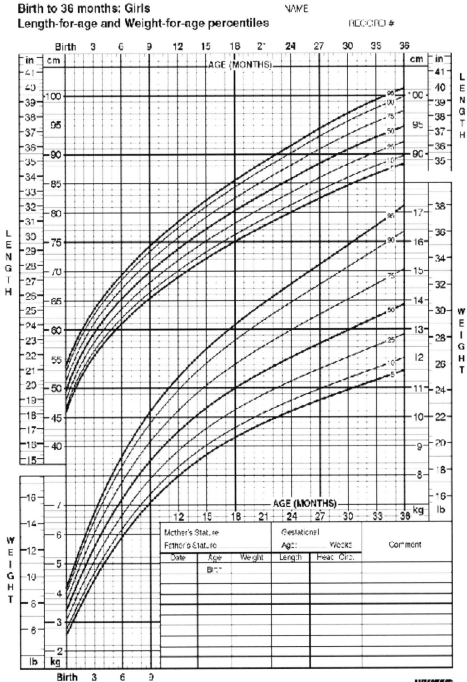

Published May 30, 2000 (modified 4/20/01).
SOURCE: Developed by the National Center for Health Statistics in collaboration with
the National Center for Chronic Disease Prevention and Health Promotion (2000).
http://www.cdc.gov/growthcharts

SAFER · HEALTHIER · PEOPLE™

Birth to 36 months: Boys
Head circumference-for-age and
Weight-for-length percentiles

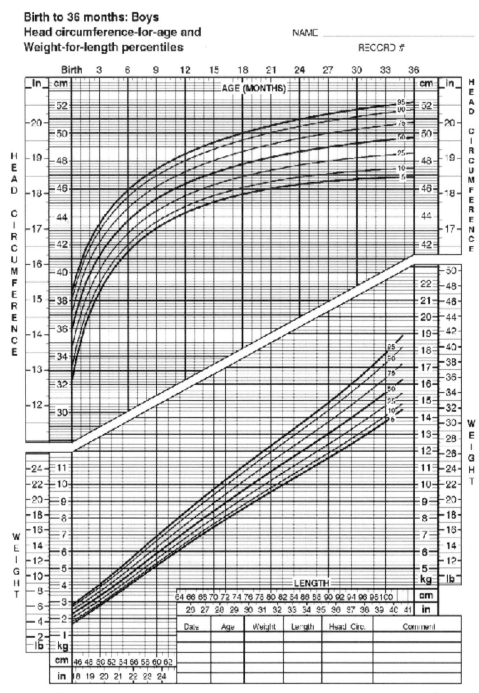

Published May 30, 2000 (modified 10/16/00).
SOURCE: Developed by the National Center for Health Statistics in collaboration with
the National Center for Chronic Disease Prevention and Health Promotion (2000).
http://www.cdc.gov/growthcharts

Birth to 36 months: Girls
Head circumference-for-age and
Weight-for-length percentiles

NAME _____

RECORD # _____

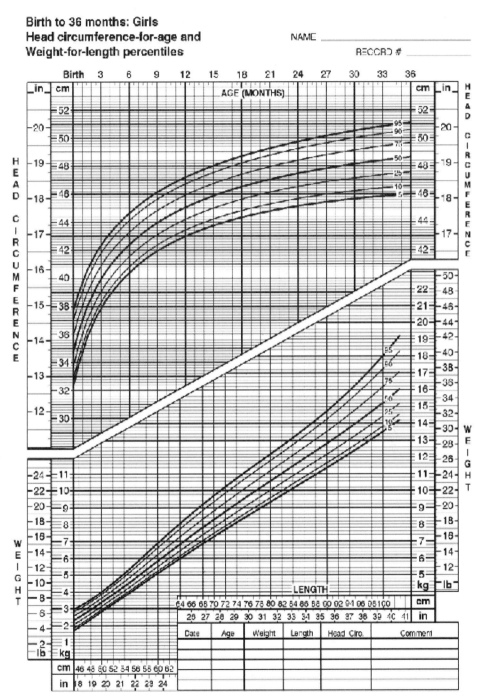

Published May 30, 2000 (modified 10/16/00).
SOURCE: Developed by the National Center for Health Statistics in collaboration with
the National Center for Chronic Disease Prevention and Health Promotion (2000).
https://www.cdc.gov/growthcharts

SAFER · HEALTHIER · PEOPLE™

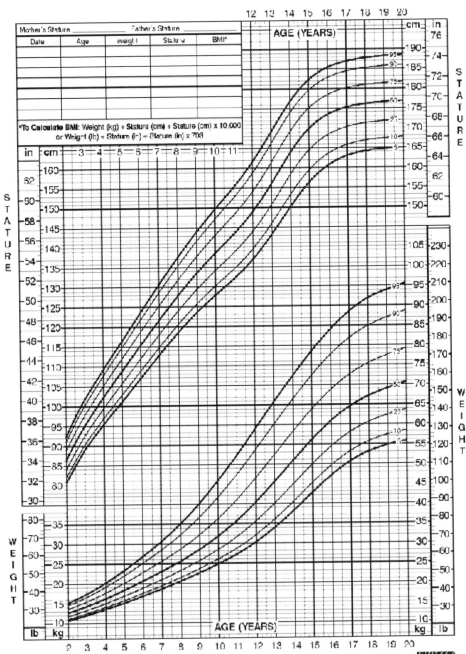

2 to 20 years: Boys
Stature-for-age and Weight-for-age percentiles

NAME _____

RECORD # _____

Published May 30, 2000 (modified 11/21/00).
SOURCE: Developed by the National Center for Health Statistics in collaboration with
the National Center for Chronic Disease Prevention and Health Promotion (2000).
http://www.cdc.gov/growthcharts

SAFER · HEALTHIER · PEOPLE

2 to 20 years: Girls
Stature-for-age and Weight-for-age percentiles

NAME

RECORD #

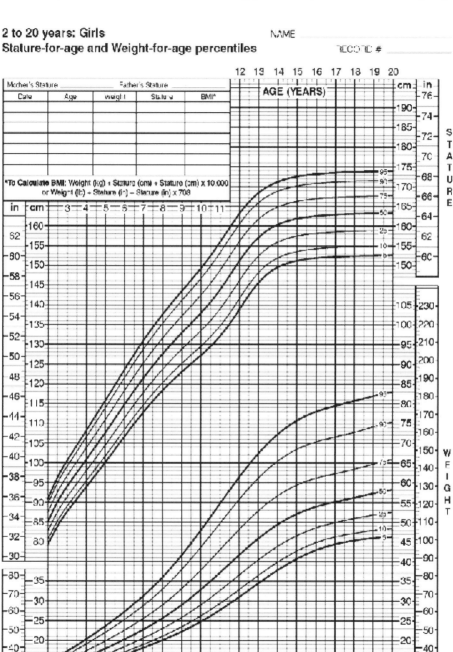

SAFER · HEALTHIER · PEOPLE™

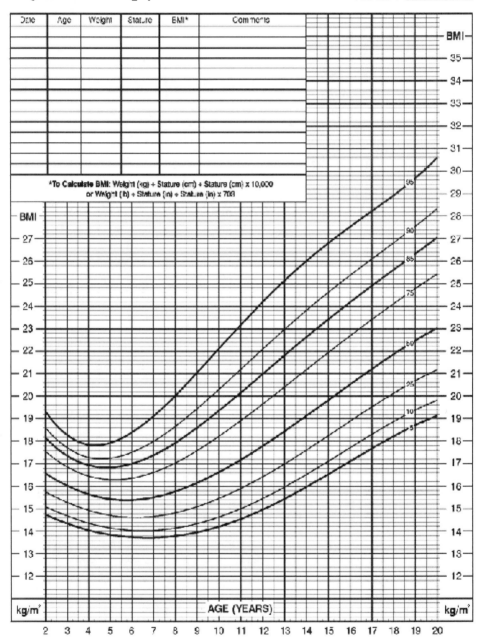

2 to 20 years: Boys
Body mass index-for-age percentiles

NAME _____

RECORD # _____

2 to 20 years: Girls
Body mass index-for-age percentiles

NAME

RECORD # _____

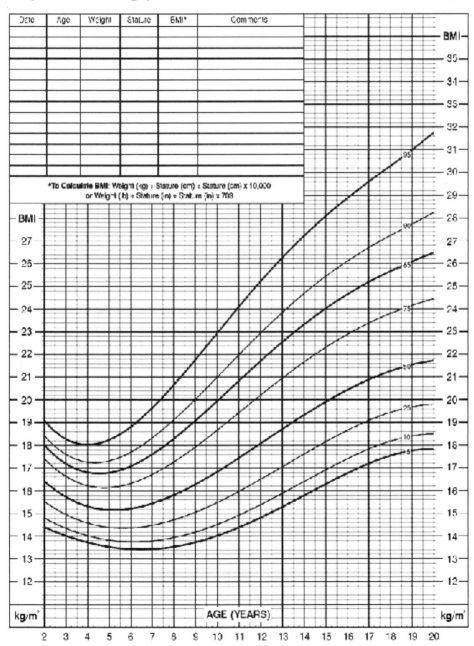

*To Calculate BMI: Weight (kg) ÷ Stature (cm) ÷ Stature (cm) x 10,000
or Weight (lb) ÷ Stature (in) ÷ Stature (in) x 703

Published May 30, 2000 (modified 12/16/00)
SOURCE: Developed by the National Center for Health Statistics in collaboration with
the National Center for Chronic Disease Prevention and Health Promotion (2000)
http://www.cdc.gov/growthcharts

SAFER·HEALTHIER·PEOPLE™

Weight-for-stature percentiles: Boys

NAME _____

RECORD # _____

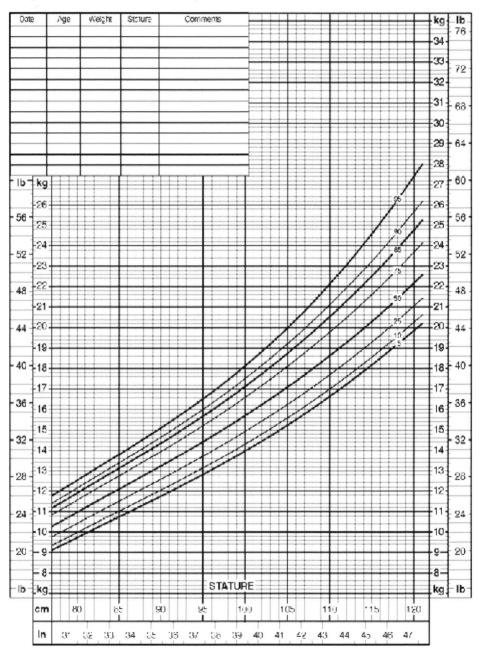

Published May 30, 2000 (modified 10/16/00).
SOURCE Developed by the National Center for Health Statistics in collaboration with
the National Center for Chronic Disease Prevention and Health Promotion (2000).
http://www.cdc.gov/growthcharts

Weight-for-stature percentiles: Girls

NAME _____

RECORD # _____

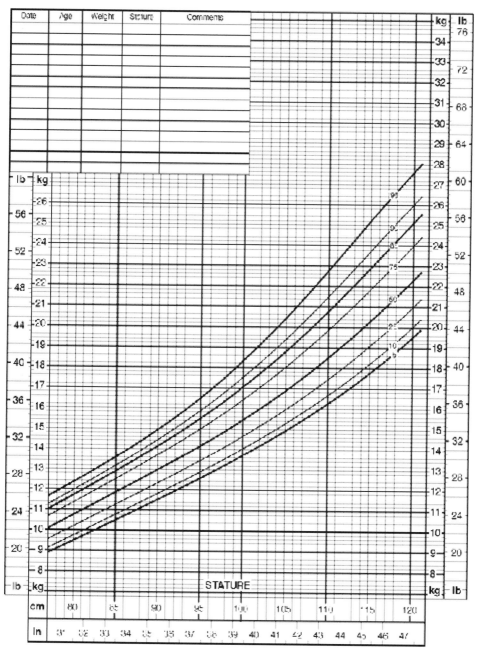

Date	Age	Weight	Stature	Comments

STATURE

Published May 30, 2000 (modified 10/16/00).

SOURCE: Developed by the National Center for Health Statistics in collaboration with the National Center for Chronic Disease Prevention and Health Promotion (2000).
http://www.cdc.gov/growthcharts

SAFER·HEALTHIER·PEOPLE™

p a r t

VI

Suggested Reading

1) *Caring for Your Baby and Young Child: Birth to Age Five.* Robert E. Hannemann, M.D. and Steven P. Shelov, M.D. 1995. American Academy of Pediatrics Press.

2) *Caring for Your School-Aged Child: Ages Five to Twelve.* Edward L. Schlor, M.D. 1995. American Academy of Pediatrics Press.

3) *Caring for Your Adolescent: Ages Twelve to Twenty one.* Donald E. Greydanus, M.D. 1991. American Academy of Pediatrics Press.

4) *The Challenge of Parenthood.* Radolf Dreikurs, M.D. 1958. Hawthorn Books, New York.

Parenting is an underdeveloped skill. There is no formal training. Traditionally, this skill was passed from generation to generation through observation, coaching, and direct modeling. Fast-moving, modern families do not have the advantage of the accumulated wisdom of several generations, handed down through the grandparents. They turn to the professionals.

Primary care pediatricians are often involved in the discussion of parenting issues with concerned families. Because of their understanding of child development and child psychology, they are uniquely suited to guide parents through difficult issues on parenting.

This book summarized the experience of a pediatric practice, trying to address some of the common issues on parenting.

Notes:

Notes:

Notes:

Notes:

Notes:

Notes:

Notes: